The Pastoral Letters have often been marginalised in modern New Testament studies. They have been regarded as not authentically Pauline, not very theological, and mostly evidence of the church settling down in the world; their patriarchal orientation has more recently further alienated readers. Yet it was these little letters which mediated Paul to the Patristic church, and then provided scriptural material for debate about church order and ministry from the Reformation to the present. This study attempts to read the Pastorals in their original setting, revising many standard scholarly assessments in the light of recent work (especially developments in sociological study of the New Testament), and exploring the gestation of a tradition which proves to be theological in its fundamental structure and its mode of addressing practical and organisational issues. The question of how texts so rooted in a different social context can be appropriated is sharply posed and addressed by the author.

D0139895

NEW TESTAMENT THEOLOGY

General Editor: James D. G. Dunn,
Lightfoot Professor of Divinity, University of Durham

The theology of the Pastoral Letters

This series provides a programmatic survey of the individual writings of the New Testament. It aims to remedy the deficiency of available published material, which has tended to concentrate on historical, textual, grammatical and literary issues at the expense of the theology, or to lose distinctive emphases of individual writings in systematised studies of 'The Theology of Paul' and the like. New Testament specialists here write at greater length than is usually possible in the introductions to commentaries or as part of other New Testament theologies, and explore the theological themes and issues of their chosen books without being tied to a commentary format, or to a thematic structure drawn from elsewhere. When complete, the series will cover all the New Testament writings, and will thus provide an attractive, and timely, range of texts around which courses can be developed.

THE THEOLOGY OF
THE PASTORAL LETTERS

FRANCES YOUNG

Edward Cadbury Professor of Theology,
University of Birmingham

CAMBRIDGE
UNIVERSITY PRESS

Published by the Press Syndicate of the University of Cambridge
The Pitt Building, Trumpington Street, Cambridge CB2 1RP
40 West 20th Street, New York, NY 10011–4211, USA
10 Stamford Road, Oakleigh, Melbourne 3166, Australia

© Cambridge University Press 1994

First published 1994

Library of Congress cataloguing in publication data

Young, Frances M. (Frances Margaret)
The theology of the Pastoral Letters / Frances Young.
p.   cm. – (New Testament theology)
Includes bibliographical references and index.
ISBN 0 521 37036 1. – ISBN 0 521 37931 8 (pbk)
1. Bible. N.T. Pastoral Epistles – Theology.
I. Title. II. Series.
BS2735.2.Y68   1994
227′.8306–dc20   93–32146 CIP

ISBN 0 521 37036 1 hardback
ISBN 0 521 37931 8 paperback

Transferred to digital printing 2004

CE

Contents

Editor's preface

Although the New Testament is usually taught within Departments or Schools or Faculties of Theology/Divinity/Religion, theological study of the individual New Testament writings is often minimal or at best patchy. The reasons for this are not hard to discern.

For one thing, the traditional style of studying a New Testament document is by means of straight exegesis, often verse by verse. Theological concerns jostle with interesting historical, textual, grammatical and literary issues, often at the cost of the theological. Such exegesis is usually very time-consuming, so that only one or two key writings can be treated in any depth within a crowded three-year syllabus.

For another, there is a marked lack of suitable textbooks round which courses could be developed. Commentaries are likely to lose theological comment within a mass of other detail in the same way as exegetical lectures. The section on the theology of a document in the Introduction to a commentary is often very brief and may do little more than pick out elements within the writing under a sequence of headings drawn from systematic theology. Excursuses usually deal with only one or two selected topics. Likewise larger works on New Testament Theology usually treat Paul's letters as a whole and, having devoted the great bulk of their space to Jesus, Paul and John, can spare only a few pages for others.

In consequence, ·there is little incentive on the part of teacher or student to engage with a particular New Testament document, and students have to be content with a general overview, at best complemented by in-depth study of (parts of) two or three New Testament writings. A serious corollary to this is the degree to which students are thereby incapacitated in the task of integrating their New Testament study with the rest of their Theology or Religion courses, since often they are capable only of drawing on the general overview or on a sequence of particular verses treated atomistically. The growing importance of a literary-critical approach to individual documents simply highlights the present deficiencies even more. Having been given little experience in handling individual New Testament writings as such at a theological level, most students are very ill-prepared to develop a properly integrated literary and theological response to particular texts. Ordinands too need more help than they currently receive from textbooks, so that their preaching from particular passages may be better informed theologically.

There is need therefore for a series to bridge the gap between too brief an introduction and too full a commentary where theological discussion is lost among too many other concerns. It is our aim to provide such a series. That is, a series where New Testament specialists are able to write at a greater length on the theology of individual writings than is usually possible in the introductions to commentaries or as part of New Testament Theologies, and to explore the theological themes and issues of these writings without being tied to a commentary format or to a thematic structure provided from elsewhere. The volumes seek both to describe each document's theology, and to engage theologically with it, noting also its canonical context and any specific influence it may have had on the history of Christian faith and life. They are directed at those who already have one or two years of full-time New Testament and theological study behind them.

University of Durham   JAMES D. G. DUNN

Abbreviations

BJRL	*Bulletin of the John Rylands Library*
ET	English translation
HUT	*Hermeneutische Untersuchungen zur Theologie*
JBL	*Journal of Biblical Literature*
JSNT	*Journal for the Study of the New Testament*
JSOT	*Journal for the Study of the Old Testament*
JTS	*Journal of Theological Studies*
NTS	*New Testament Studies*
SBL	Society of Biblical Literature
SNTS	Society for New Testament Studies
TDNT	*Theological Dictionary of the New Testament*
WUNT	*Wissenschaftliche Untersuchungen zum Neuen Testament*

CHAPTER 1

Theology and its context

INTRODUCTION

Theology is always earthed in a context. Over the centuries, Christian theologians have tried to construct theological systems which they have believed to be eternal, but in practice the statement of theological truths has to be constantly revised, because human language, human cultures, human philosophies, etc. are all subject to change, and in the end theology has to be articulated for human beings in human concepts.

This is not to pre-judge the issue of the source of revelation.[1] If the Christian claim that God has revealed the divine self has any validity, then God has accommodated that revelation to human circumstances, using human language, coming in human form. One of the key claims of the Christian tradition is that God has been concerned with the particularities of human existence. Christian theology therefore has to take seriously the particular historical context of those documents which are believed to be God's Word, and also the particular context in which those documents are being interpreted.

If that is true for the New Testament in general, it is especially acute for the interpreter of the so-called Pastoral epistles.[2] This title is used for the three little letters which

---

[1] Two recent discussions may be recommended: my own book, *The Art of Performance* (London, 1990); and Sandra Schneiders, *The Revelatory Text: Interpreting the New Testament as Sacred Scripture* (San Francisco, 1991). See further chapter 7.

[2] This designation seems to have originated with P. Anton in 1726. It is generally held to describe their character as address to 'pastors' concerning the shepherding of their churches.

1

appear to be written by the Apostle Paul to his helpers,
Timothy and Titus. However, it seems these letters were slower
than others coming into use in the second century, and their
contents strongly suggest that to accept that attribution is to
misread the setting and purpose of these texts. So there are
problems with discerning the particular historical context of
these documents. There are also problems for the context of the
modern Christian reader. To a fair extent the teaching in these
epistles seems very culture-specific, concerned as they are with
the practical outworking of Christian living at the time and in
the social environment in which they were written.
Unquestionably, women readers have found much here that
has tended to marginalise them in the structures of churches
which believe their organisation to be based on scripture in
general and the Pastorals in particular. The problems related
to both contexts, that of writer and reader, will have to be
addressed.

But there is another problem of New Testament Theology
which is particularly acute in the case of the Pastorals. These
documents are not theological treatises, and the theology is
often implicit rather than explicit. It has even been seriously
suggested that the Pastorals have very little theology, and that
would seem to make the project of this book impossible.
However, any attempt to read these letters soon runs up
against the fact that they come from a particular social context
in which there is an encompassing theological perspective
which colours all the material which at first sight appears to be
ethical or practical rather than theological in its principal
thrust. To discuss the theology of the Pastorals is therefore to
engage in a reconstruction not only of their context but of their
tradition. Explicitly there is a lack of theological concern, but
their fundamentally theological character may be seen in the
way they map out life lived under God.

The problem with reconstructing context and tradition is
that the evidence for embarking on this consists largely of the
texts themselves. Of course a certain amount can be gained by
comparison with other texts, whether from the immediate
period, or texts which we know would have been influential,
such as the Jewish scriptures. These can provide access to the

kind of culture, inbuilt assumptions and linguistic community which is likely to have formed the mind of the author and the original readers. In the case of the Pastorals such comparison is particularly important, especially comparison with other early Christian literature, not least the letters of Paul, for the relationship between these three brief letters and the other evidence we have about early Christianity can alone help to determine their date, background and tradition. Yet we cannot entirely escape from the problem that reconstructing context and tradition depends on reading the very texts that we wish to elucidate through that reconstruction. This creates a problem of method. It is all too easy to set up an interpretative framework in advance which then determines how the texts are read.

But there is a sense in which providing an outline of the theology of these epistles implies that conclusions have been reached on the basis of reading and re-reading the texts, taking account of the circularity involved. That circularity I would prefer to regard as spiralling, in the sense that each attempt at reconstruction is provisional and subject to revision as a result of re-reading, and each re-reading is illuminated by the cumulative process of piecing together the clues. So in accordance with the shape of other studies in this series, this opening chapter will attempt to show how and why these epistles are placed in a certain historical context. The subsequent chapters will relate both the explicit and the implicit theological content of the epistles to that context, in the process both illuminating and to some extent confirming the hypothetical reconstruction. It is not intended, however, simply to read these epistles as historical documents; so the final chapters consider their reception within the Christian tradition, and how there can be an appropriate reading of them as scripture in the different socio-cultural environment of present-day readers.

THE ORIGINAL READERS

The texts invite us to suppose that the recipients of these letters were Timothy and Titus, one being addressed to the latter, two to the former. Quite quickly, however, we are left a little puzzled. What we find in 1 Timothy and Titus (2 Timothy is somewhat different) is a collection of instructions about ordering the belief and life of the church which, on the one hand, seem to be adapted 'household codes', and on the other hand, anticipate later church orders and collections of canons. These later collections of church instructions, like the *Didachē*, the *Didascalia Apostolorum* and the *Apostolic Constitutions*,[3] invariably attribute their origins to Apostles, but clearly all developed over time as community manuals. The texts with which we are concerned, namely the Pastorals, also appear to have a community in view rather than an individual, to be public not private communications, presented as having the apostolic authority of Paul.[4]

But the community's tradition is in this case cast in a form that also presents Timothy and Titus as its authoritative mediators from Paul. Yet they are characterized as in the authentic Pauline letters or the narrative of Acts, despite the supposed situation being new and different, probably later. So where Timothy the individual is addressed, sometimes he is

[3] The *Didachē* (*The Teaching of the Twelve Apostles*) was regarded by some in the third century as part of the canon of scripture, but was later lost. It was rediscovered in 1883. Many think that it has a 'primitive' character and belongs to the first century; others regard its primitiveness as 'contrived' and place it in the second. Whatever the date of its compilation, it certainly contains material from earlier times and probably of various dates. It was put together as a compendium of what we might call 'church conventions' and is usually described as 'a rudimentary manual of church order' (Simon Tugwell, *The Apostolic Fathers* (London 1989)). It is easily accessible in the Penguin translation, *Early Christian Writings*, by Maxwell Staniforth and Andrew Louth (revised, London, 1987). Its content was incorporated into later collections of canons, such as the *Didascalia Apostolorum* and the *Apostolic Constitutions*. The *Didascalia* (*The Catholic Teaching of the Twelve Apostles and Holy Disciples of our Saviour*) probably comes from Syria and was compiled in the early third century; the original Greek is lost but it survives complete in Syriac and other versions: see R. H. Connolly, *Didascalia Apostolorum: The Syriac Version Translated and Accompanied by the Verona Latin Fragments* (Oxford, 1929). The *Apostolic Constitutions* (ET in the Ante-Nicene Christian Library, vol. XVII (Edinburgh, 1870)) is the largest collections of legislative and liturgical material, the first six books being an edited and expanded version of the material in the *Didascalia*, the seventh an enlargement of the *Didachē*, and the eighth using as its source another earlier work known as *The Apostolic Tradition* of (Ps.-) Hippolytus. The collection probably dates from the late fourth century. These examples are the most important instances of what was clearly a developing and expanding collection of 'canonical traditions'.

[4] Norbert Brox, *Die Pastoralbriefe*, Regensburger Neues Testament 7.2 (Regensburg, 1969), pp. 11–12, emphasises the official character of these documents. They are concerned with discipline, and present exemplary, authoritative, apostolic instruction.

treated as the bearer of a tradition with considerable authority to root out false teaching (e.g. 1.3ff.; 4.6ff.), sometimes as the youngster assistant who needs to have his authority enhanced, is singularly ignorant of fairly elementary matters and even has to be told rather well-known things about his master, Paul (e.g. 4.12; 6.11ff.; 1.12ff. and 2 Tim.). Titus is less well characterised, but also seems to need surprising reminders if he really held the position attributed to him.

Thus the implied readership, as distinct from the stated readership, seems to be a Christian community or communities somewhere, sometime in the first (or possibly early second) century, for which Paul's authority is important and believed to have been transmitted through his close personal assistants, Timothy and Titus. The implication that these texts carry is that the original 'seniors' (presbyters) and leaders of the community received appointment from Paul's envoys.

THE SITUATION OF THE COMMUNITY (-IES)

One only has to read the opening verses of the body of the first letter to Timothy to realise that at the time when these texts were produced there was grave concern about 'false teaching'. The nature of that false teaching is hinted at, but remains somewhat elusive because, unlike Paul, in Galatians for example, the texts do not address the issues or confute them by argument; rather the falsity of the opposing teachings is simply asserted, and particular practices enjoined upon any community which intends to remain faithful to the approved tradition. That may in itself provide some clues, but the reconstruction of the context is not absolutely straightforward. We must consider the possibilities and the grounds on which a particular reconstruction may be recommended.

Let us begin by noting what these three letters actually say about the false teaching:

1 Timothy 1.1–7

The false teachers apparently devote themselves to interminable myths and genealogies, regarded by this text as simply generating speculation. They go astray into a wilderness of words. They set out to be teachers of the law, though they do not understand the words they use or the subjects about which they are so dogmatic.

1 Timothy 1.19–20

Assuming these verses refer to the same people, two are named as Hymenaeus and Alexander; they are said to have made shipwreck of their faith, and it is implied that 'Paul' regarded their teaching as blasphemous. Probably the same Hymenaeus appears in 2 Timothy 2.17, though there his name is coupled with a certain Philetus.

1 Timothy 4.1–7

It is clearly believed that the Spirit foretold that some would forsake the faith and surrender their minds to subversive spirits and demon-inspired doctrines. This suggests that the false teaching is recognised to be a perversion of the truth, rather than totally alien to it. The falsehoods sound only too plausible because they are close to what the tradition has taught. We are now told that the false teachers forbid marriage and insist on abstinence from foods which God created to be enjoyed with thanksgiving. A strong ascetic bent is implied. Again warning is offered against superstitious myths and old wives' tales. It is not altogether clear whether there is any connection between such old-wives' tales and the gossiping of younger unmarried widows mentioned in 5.11–13, though some connection may be hinted at in the fact that there the young widows are un-married and here the condemnation of marriage is forbidden.

1 Timothy 6.3ff. and 20

Again those who teach and preach other than sound precepts are described as having a morbid enthusiasm for mere specu-lations and quibbles. They are charged with causing jealousy, slander, suspicion and division in the community, and with expecting that religion should yield dividends, the implication being that it provides some kind of profit, for the next verses speak of the love of money and the proper use of riches.[5] Finally 'Timothy' is advised to turn a deaf ear to empty and irreligious chatter, and the contradictions of 'knowledge falsely so-called'.

2 Timothy 2.14ff.

People are to be charged not to dispute about mere words. 'Timothy' is to avoid empty and irreligious chatter. False teaching is like an infection, spreading like gangrene. Hymenaeus appears again, this time with Philetus. So far we seem justified in assuming that the same group is in view. Now we learn something new: these people are associated with the view that the resurrection has happened already. 'Timothy' is to have nothing to do with foolish and wild speculations because they generate battles.

2 Timothy 3

As we move into the next chapter, we seem to find all this associated with the final eschatological turmoil as the end of the world approaches. Emphasis is placed on love of self and money, on pride and self-importance, scandalmongering and hatred, loving pleasures more than God. These people preserve the outward form of religion, but are a denial of its power. But are they the false teachers? Their 'lack of control' seems somewhat incompatible with the asceticism we found earlier (the Greek *akrateis* is the opposite of 'encratite', a word used later for extreme ascetics). Yet the love of money, the pride and the divisiveness seem recognisable, and as we go on we find that they insinuate themselves into private houses and lead astray

---

[5] This range of charges may reflect standard motifs of vilification; see Robert J. Karris, 'The Background and Significance of the Polemic of the Pastoral Epistles', *JBL* 92 (1973), 549–64. The view of Dibelius–Conzelmann is substantiated with detailed evidence, though Karris usefully distinguishes features of the opponents from the predominantly 'stock' descriptions.

gullible women. Does this perhaps imply the same situation as was implied in 1 Tim. 4.7 and 5.13?

These people are compared with Jannes and Jambres, the legendary opponents of Moses. Their names do not appear in the Jewish scriptures, but are found in many Jewish texts of the Hellenistic period.[6] Since they were two of Pharaoh's magicians, the comparison may imply charges of sorcery, but the explicit point made is that they oppose the truth. Their minds are warped and their foolishness will eventually be exposed. Perhaps the false teachers are also in view when it is suggested that while persecution will come to every true believer, evil doers and charlatans will progress from bad to worse, deceiving and deceived.

Those criticised would seem to bear comparison with the false teachers in 1 Timothy despite the curious differences noted.

2 Timothy 4.3–4.

The context is again the Final Judgment and end-time, and the time is predicted when people will not stand sound teaching but will all follow their own whim and gather a crowd of teachers to tickle their fancy, stopping their ears to the truth and turning to fables. These verses seem to confirm that 2 Timothy has the same opponents in view as 1 Timothy (e.g. 4.1–7).[7]

Titus 1.10ff

These verses follow an injunction to 'sound teaching', and contrast certain Jewish converts who are undisciplined, talk wildly and lead others astray. Such people have to be silenced. It is suggested that they do it for gain, which is a point already noted in the letters to Timothy.

---

[6] Exod 7.8ff. and 9.11 refer to Pharaoh's magicians but do not name them. For witnesses to this unwritten Jewish tradition, see Dibelius–Conzelmann, *The Pastoral Epistles*(ET Philadelphia, 1972), p. 117.

[7] See above, p. 6.

Curiously it is then implied that the false teachers are Cretans, for the universally known proverb, 'All Cretans are liars' is used against them.[8] This letter purports to be addressed to Titus in Crete, so geographically this suits, though it may not immediately seem compatible with the statement that they are Jews, or with their similarity to the false teachers of the letters to Timothy who is supposed to be in Ephesus. If the false teachers represent a widespread movement, however, the geography may present no problems, and we should not forget that Acts presents Jews from the Diaspora on pilgrimage to Jerusalem calling themselves Parthians, Medes, Elamites ... Cretans and Arabs (2.9–11).

Anyway, these presumably local disrupters are to be rebuked and restored to a sound faith, instead of paying heed to Jewish myths and 'human commandments', presumably a less than respectful reference to the Jewish law. These comments marry well with the opening description in 1 Timothy which associates teaching the law with interest in myths, though many scholars have found this association problematic when it comes to identifying the false teachers.

Titus 3.9–11

An injunction to avoid foolish speculations, genealogies, quarrels and controversies over the law again reminds us of the first letter to Timothy (1 Tim. 1.1–7; 6.3ff.), as does the warning against those who are contentious, and the reference to having a distorted mind.

Surveying this material, we note two points which have produced a certain puzzlement: firstly, the association of concern with the law, or 'human commandments' in the writer's view, with myths, speculations and genealogies, and the association of the latter with Jews; secondly, the apparent contradiction

---

[8] The proverb was attributed to Epimenides of Cnossos in Crete, one of the 'seven wise men' of Greek antiquity (sixth century BC), described as a prophet by Plato, Aristotle and Cicero. The saying was so well known that *krētizein* (to Cretise) was a slang word for lying or cheating, and a famous logical puzzle was: if a Cretan says all Cretans are liars, how can it be true?

between the charges concerned with money-grubbing and pleasures and the implication that the false teachers encouraged a radical asceticism in both diet and sexual relations. Each of these requires consideration.

(1) The phrase '*gnōsis* falsely so-called' (1 Tim. 6.20) came to be used by the church Fathers as a description of that family of heresies modern scholarship has named 'gnosticism',[9] and the myths and genealogies have therefore been widely interpreted as referring to cosmological schemata such as are found in the gnostic systems of the second century, the 'families of descending emanations, or aeons, by which they [i.e. the gnostics like Valentinus] bridged the gulf between the unknowable supreme God and the material order'.[10] Such systems, it used to be thought,[11] arose from the 'radical Hellenization' of Christianity. So the phrase 'Jewish myths' (Titus 1.14) and the association with 'Jewish converts' seemed on the face of it somewhat problematic. Even more curious was the apparent interest in the Jewish law.

This apparent discrepancy led some scholars to challenge the notion that gnosticism was in view. The genealogies, it was suggested,[12] are to do with Jewish Haggadic interest in the genealogies of the scriptures, the sort of thing found in the book of Jubilees, and so they concluded that the problems were

[9] The most comprehensive recent survey of what is one of the most debated subjects in modern scholarship is provided by Kurt Rudolph, *Gnosis* (ET Edinburgh, 1983). An alternative perspective is provided by Simone Pétrement, *A Separate God: The Christian Origins of Gnosticism* (ET London, 1991). Earlier useful works include R. McL. Wilson, *The Gnostic Problem* (London, 1958); R. M. Grant, *Gnosticism and Early Christianity* (London 1959); E. M. Yamauchi, *Pre-Christian Gnosticism* (London, 1973).

[10] Quoted from J. N. D. Kelly, *The Pastoral Epistles*, Black's New Testament Commentaries (London, 1963), p. 44.

[11] Harnack's much-quoted description, in his *History of Dogma* at the turn of the century, was 'the acute Hellenization of Christianity'.

[12] E.g. E. F. Scott, *The Pastoral Epistles*, The Moffatt New Testament Commentary (London, 1936), pp. 8ff.; of other English commentators, Kelly is sympathetic, but the idea is contested by C. K. Barrett, *The Pastoral Epistles*, New Clarendon Bible (Oxford, 1963), and A. T. Hanson, *The Pastoral Epistles*, The New Century Bible Commentary (London, 1982). Dibelius–Conzelmann also reject the theory, referring to German discussions. The Book of Jubilees can be found in J. H. Charlesworth (ed.), *The Old Testament Pseudepigrapha: Apocalyptic Literature and Testaments*, vol. II (London, 1983).

related, not to gnosticism at all, but to the Judaising issue and speculative exegesis of the scriptures. This makes the association with interest in the Jewish law entirely natural. It also challenges one argument for dating these epistles as late as the early second century.

Meanwhile, however, scholarly understanding of gnosticism has advanced, and it is now widely believed that, however syncretistic its tendencies within the Hellenistic environment, its roots, like the roots of Christianity itself, may well have been in apocalyptic Judaism.[13] Indeed, Jewish Christianity, it is suspected, had gnostic tendencies. Many[14] have argued that gnosticism or proto-gnosticism was already affecting Paul's converts in Corinth, and certainly Colossians[15] seems to imply something similar to the teaching that is so problematic in the Pastorals. This is another reason for recognising that association with the second-century gnostic systems is unnecessary. Here, then, the problem of the background to the Pastorals relates to continuing discussions about the background and development of both Judaism and Christianity in the first and early second centuries. What is evident is that the association of Jewish and gnostic elements can be paralleled elsewhere and there is no need to regard this as problematic, or to attempt to posit more than one opposition.

That said, however, the Pastorals do seem to reflect a stage in the development of Jewish gnostic ideas which is somewhere between that associated with Cerinthus, a notorious early gnostic said to have been avoided by John, the disciple of the Lord, in the bath-house at Ephesus,[16] and that faced by Igna-

---

[13] A pioneering study was R. M. Grant, *Gnosticism and Early Christianity* (New York, 1966). Cf. Christopher Rowland, *The Open Heaven* (London, 1982).

[14] Notably W. Schmithals, *Gnosticism in Corinth* (ET Nashville, 1971).

[15] This view has been a major factor in the challenge to Pauline authorship of Colossians, as for the Pastorals: see, e.g. W. G. Kummel, *Introduction to the New Testment* (ET London, 1966).

[16] Eusebius, *Historia Ecclesiastica* III.28.6, reporting Polycarp. In the great compendia of heresies written by, e.g., Irenaeus (late second century) and Epiphanius (mid-fourth century), Cerinthus, with Menander, provides the link between Simon Magus, identified with Simon in Acts 8.9–24, and later heresiarchs like Basilides and Valentinus. Eusebius' disapproving account suggests that Cerinthus expected after the resurrection a literal kingdom-banquet in Jerusalem – indeed 1,000 years

tius, bishop of Antioch in the early second century,[17] rather than that reflected in first-century material such as the unquestionably authentic Pauline letters. In other words, despite the tantalisingly meagre information on all sides, it would seem likely that the situation implied by the Pastorals is pushing towards the second century rather than fitting easily into Paul's lifetime.

The reaction against developing gnosticism seems to have taken the form of a reaffirmation of eschatological expectation (e.g. the Johannine epistles), and in the second century, the Christian 'mainstream', as recognised later by hindsight, seems to have favoured millenarian ideas (e.g. Papias[18]). It is not surprising, then, to find these texts associating false teachers with prophecies about the *eschaton* (2 Tim. 3.1ff.), nor is the hint implausible that unlike true believers these misguided people avoid persecution (2 Tim. 3.12); Ignatius suggests that his sacrificial martyrdom is undermined by the docetic teachings he opposes. Gnostics (though not, it seems, Cerinthus, who is said to have had expectations of a millenarian kind) are associated with the idea that the resurrection is spiritual and has therefore already happened in the lives of believers. Also later anti-gnostic polemic charged certain teachers with insinuating themselves into households, misleading women and

of wedding-feasts! However, Irenaeus suggests that his beliefs were less apocalyptic and more gnostic: the world was not made by the primary God, but a lesser Power, and the human Jesus was distinct from the Christ which descended on him at baptism.

[17] In the extant authentic letters of Ignatius, it used to be thought that two different heresies were being addressed, gnosticising and Judaising. A similar reassessment has taken place, though the two problems appear in distinct letters. W. R. Schoedel in his commentary on Ignatius in the Hermeneia series (Philadelphia, 1985) suggests that there is no coherent movement to which Ignatius is opposed; rather he polarises the issue with local Christians with whom he happens to disagree. The fact that parallel conflicts are found internally in the church in other documents suggests that while local ferment may be the immediate issue, wider tendencies contribute (as now in the case of local conflicts stimulated by the charismatic movement).

[18] Eusebius, *Historia Ecclesiastica* III.39, uses Papias of Hierapolis, a contemporary of Polycarp and Ignatius, as a source for second-century reports concerning the gospels, but he regarded him as a 'man of small intelligence', largely it would seem because he said in his books 'that after the resurrection of the dead there will be a period of a thousand years, when Christ's kingdom will be set up on this earth in material form'.

doing it for the money. It is easy to recognise gnostic characteristics in the false teachers of the Pastorals, as indeed Irenaeus[19]
did in the late second century.

(2) Some gnostics seem to have deduced from their deni-
gration of the flesh the practice of a strict asceticism, others,
licence to indulge the flesh since it was irrelevant to their
spiritual salvation. But it would seem unlikely that these two
views should co-exist among the same false teachers. In the
Pastorals, extreme asceticism seems to be repudiated both
explicitly and by implication: teaching against marriage is
condemned, Timothy is advised to take a little wine for his
stomach, and food provided by the Creator is to be received
with thanksgiving. Yet excess is also to be avoided, as is evident
in the many injunctions as to how church leaders are to
conduct themselves, soberly, with temperance and *enkrateia*
(see above), and the false teachers are possibly accused of
loving money and pleasures. How are these tensions in the
description of the opposition to be resolved?

It could be that preoccupation with gnosticism has blinded
scholarship until recently to those features of early Christianity
which most naturally make sense of the stance of the Pastorals.
More recent interest in social norms and organisation may
have pointed to more fruitful contexts for understanding some
aspects of the situation to which these letters were addressed.[20]

Not all apocryphal literature bears the gnostic stamp, and
some of it was valued in the church even as it failed to reach
canonical status. Such a work was the Acts of Paul. In the third
century, the work was used by people like Hippolytus and
Origen without qualm, though treated as disputed by the time
of Eusebius. Its early date is assured by Tertullian, whose

[19] Bishop of Lyons and first writer to create an anti-heretical encyclopedia, largely
concerned to trace the history of gnostic error. Prior to modern discoveries such as
the Nag Hammadi library, Irenaeus and his successors, Hippolytus and Epiphanius, were our principal sources for gnostic teaching.

[20] The work which stimulated new approaches was D. R. MacDonald, *The Legend and
the Apostle: The Battle for Paul in Story and Canon* (Philadelphia, 1983). He argued that
the Pastorals were written to counter oral stories and legends about Paul of the kind
which were collected into the Acts of Paul later. This was taken up by Margaret Y.
Macdonald, *The Pauline Churches: A Socio-historical Study of Institutionalization in the
Pauline and Deutero-Pauline Writings*, SNTS Monograph Series (Cambridge, 1988).

mention of a particular section of it is apposite to our discussion:

If those who read the writings that falsely bear the name of Paul adduce the example of Thecla to maintain the right of women to teach and to baptize, let them know that the presbyter in Asia who produced this document, as if he could of himself add anything to the prestige of Paul, was removed from his office after he had been convicted and had confessed that he did it out of love for Paul.[21]

The complete text of the Acts of Paul is not extant, but the section known as Acts of Paul and Thecla survived independently in a number of manuscripts and versions.

This narrative tells how Paul visited Iconium, and in the house of Onesiphorus preached about 'continence and the resurrection'.[22] There follows a series of Beatitudes quoted as the content of his teaching of which the following provide an instructive sample:

Blessed are the pure in heart for they shall see God.
Blessed are they who have kept flesh pure, for they shall become the Temple of God.
Blessed are they who have wives as if they had them not, for they shall inherit God.
Blessed are the bodies of the virgins, for they shall be well pleasing to God, and shall not lose the reward for their piety.

Listening to this preaching deeply affected a virgin named Thecla, we are told, who was already betrothed. Paul is accused of teaching falsely that resurrection depends on chastity; his opponents claim that the resurrection has already taken place, for 'we are risen again in that we have come to know the true God'. The prospective bridegroom initiates proceedings against Paul, and the narrative traces the details of imprisonment, arraignment, etc., concentrating on Thecla's infatuation with Paul's gospel of virginity and her pursuit of Paul, her near-martyrdoms (in Iconium, she was saved by a storm quenching the fire, which in any case 'did not touch her';

---

[21] *De Baptismo* 17, as quoted by W. Schneemelcher, introducing The Acts of Paul in E. Hennecke, *New Testament Apocrypha*, vol. II, ET ed. R. McL. Wilson (London, 1965), p. 323.
[22] *Ibid.*, p. 354.

in Antioch the wild beasts lay at her feet), her baptism, her adoption of the teacher's mantle and her witness for Christ.

Not only the charges against false teachers, but much else in the Pastorals begins to make sense against the background of this narrative. It seems not unlikely that the Pastorals and the Acts of Paul come from Asia Minor, and even if it is a bit optimistic to suggest they 'were composed as little as a generation apart',[23] the likelihood that the stories and legends were already popular, perhaps particularly among women, especially groups of celibate women, seems high.[24] The author of the Acts of Paul must have written in the second century (Tertullian's date is around 200 CE), and presumably collected such oral legends about Paul.

We know that Paul's teaching was controversial after his death: the author of 2 Peter warns that Paul's letters contain obscure passages, which the ignorant and unstable misinterpret to their own ruin (3.14–16), and second-century false teachers like Marcion and the gnostics seem to have claimed to represent the Pauline tradition. Indeed, it has been shown that two antithetical traditions of Pauline exegesis emerged in the late first to the second century; one read Paul anti-gnostically, the other gnostically.[25] In the apocryphal Acts, some followers of Paul, perhaps apocalyptic enthusiasts, seem to be taking too seriously his advice to remain unmarried until the coming of the Lord (2 Cor. 7). Interestingly, like the Pastorals, they are

---

[23] MacDonald, *The Pauline Churches*, p. 181.

[24] MacDonald, *The Legend of the Apostle*. We may cite a few of his many examples of links: the Christianised version of Androcles and the Lion which appears in the Acts of Paul (Hennecke and Schneemelcher, *New Testament Apocrypha*, vol. II, pp.370ff.) may be reflected in 2 Tim. 4.16–19; in both the Pastorals and the Acts of Paul, but only there, we meet a Hermogenes who deserts Paul, a companion called Demas, faithful Onesiphorus and an Alexander who opposes him; the claim that the resurrection has already happened is actually found in early Christian literature only in the Pastorals and the Acts of Paul, both of which oppose the idea.

[25] Elaine Pagels, *The Gnostic Paul: Gnostic Exegesis of the Pauline Letters* (Philadelphia, 1975, 1992). It is clear that the Valentinians identified Paul as the source of their tradition; only those who had received instruction into their secret, oral tradition were capable of understanding the true meaning of the scriptures, including Paul's epistles (Irenaeus, *Adversus Haereses* 3.2.1). Paul taught in two ways at once: he preached the Saviour according to the flesh to the psychics, or ordinary church members, but to the elect, the gnostics, he proclaimed Christ according to the spirit (Clement of Alexandria, *Excerpta ex Theodoto* 23.3–4).

opposed by people claiming that the resurrection has happened already, so the tension between gnostic spiritualising and apocalyptic enthusiasm is surely in the background.

Apocalyptic enthusiasm would encourage radical opposition to the Roman state, and the stories of the Acts of Paul 'presuppose conflict between the Roman Empire, convinced of its own legitimacy, power and permanence, and an apocalyptic sect awaiting destruction of the world. This expectation of the End provided them with a rival political vision, spawned radical social behaviour and promised divine vindication for those persecuted in the struggle.'[26] The Pastorals depart from such a radical apocalyptic stance, encouraging Christians to be law-abiding citizens, and to conform to social norms. In other words, these texts share opposition to gnosticism, but take opposing views on the issue of Christian lifestyle in the social order of the present world. All three stances seem to claim to represent the Pauline tradition.

What the Pastorals seem to find most objectionable is the disruption of households and of normal social relations caused by private teaching of the type apparently described in the Acts of Paul, by women desiring to preserve their virginity and refusing to conform to convention, and the consequent disrepute brought upon the church and its leaders. Extremism of any sort is to be rejected, perhaps in the cause of mission.[27] Proper ordering of the household of God depends on proper ordering of households in general.

That in the second century Christians were seen as subversive precisely because of activities such as those criticised in the Pastorals is evidenced in the anti-Christian treatise of Celsus, written in the mid second century and preserved for us by Origen, who wrote a detailed refutation of it point by point in the following century. Celsus stated:

In private houses also we see wool-workers, cobblers, laundry-workers, and the most illiterate and bucolic yokels, who would not dare to say anything at all in front of their elders and more intelligent

---

[26] MacDonald, *The Legend and the Apostle*, p. 40.

[27] Cf. Philip H. Towner, *The Goal of our Instruction: The Structure of Theology and Ethics in the Pastoral Epistles*, JSNT Monograph Series 34 (Sheffield, 1989). He is not aware of

masters. But whenever they get hold of children in private and some stupid women with them, they let out some astounding statements as, for example, that they must not pay attention to their father and school-teacher.[28]

A little earlier Celsus suggested that Christians were not interested in educated people, only the ignorant, slaves, women and children. His perception of Christianity is endorsed by Aelius Aristides, a rhetorician from Smyrna, who sometime between 161 and 165, lashed out at both Cynics and Christians in the same breath for flouting social conventions. They

divide and upset the household, and bring into collision those inside with each other, and tell them the worst ways to manage their household. They never say, find, or do anything socially productive. They do not participate in panegyrics (festal assemblies), nor worship the gods, nor help govern the cities, nor comfort the sorrowing, nor make reconciliation with those of opposing persuasions, nor arouse the young – or anyone else for that matter – to the affairs of the world.[29]

The Acts of Paul and Thecla present us with the world of the wealthy urban householder, with marriages arranged to forge social alliances and proper succession, with the kind of establishment that Aristotle suggested mirrored the state in its hierarchical organisation, very different from a modern nuclear family, consisting as it did of servants, slaves, clients, workers, tenants, etc. Such a social world would even have had its household gods, towards which pious duty was practised for the sake of prosperity, and might even have had a kind of philosopher chaplain. The Pastorals seek to foster a Christian version of this stable world, whereas the Acts depict it under threat, perhaps the very threat which the Pastorals attempt to obviate.

Christian leaders are to be good householders, and they should not countenance supposedly Christian teachers who

---

this potential context, but argues the general point made here about the rejection of extremism.

[28] *Contra Celsum* III.55, trans. H. Chadwick (Cambridge, 1953), p. 165.

[29] *In Defense of the Four*, 309.13–17, as quoted by MacDonald, *The Legend of the Apostle*, p. 46.

have insinuated themselves into private houses either to earn money as philosopher-chaplains or via the back-stairs, as it were. Nor should we forget that such stable households were the locus of 'house-churches', and church groups almost certainly depended on the patronage of wealthy converted householders for material support, influence and leadership. Too radical an understanding of the Christian gospel could threaten the very world on which the church depended.

The anxiety to offer proper standards of behaviour, especially for women, particularly those free of the constraints of marriage (and widowhood at an early age was far more likely at a time when expectation of life was decades lower than it has become in the modern world), is understandable against the picture of ascetic enthusiasm painted in the Acts. On the other hand, an informal network of house-churches provides the social setting in which both gnostic teachings and ascetic radicalism would easily travel.

This kind of scenario may be enough to explain the conjunction between ascetic teaching and the accusations of making profit from religion, pleasure-seeking, etc. It was all too easy to bring charges of immoral motives, whether they had any grounds or not, and later anti-heretical works would invariably do this. However, another possible factor in the social background might be a better explanation of the expectation that religion will bring reward. In the urban 'association' (*koinōnia*), which gives us something of a parallel to the early church, the well-to-do householder who provided a place of meeting and supported the group financially would expect to receive honour, influence and power as a result. Throughout ancient society there was a mutual dependence of rich and poor, patron and client, in which each offered the other support; the rich provided material benefits, while their dependants offered honour (*timē*) and glory (*doxa*), gratitude and loyalty.[30]

[30] S. C. Mott, 'Reciprocity in Hellenistic Benevolence', in E. G. Hawthorne (ed.), *Current Issues in Biblical and Patristic Interpretation*, Tenney Festschrift (Grand Rapids, 1975); cf. A. R. Hands, *Charities and Social Aid in Greece and Rome* (Grand Rapids, 1982), and Richard P. Saller, *Personal Patronage under the Early Empire* (Cambridge, 1982).

There is an important passage in the final chapter of 1 Timothy concerning the rich Christian, who is not to look for the usual reward on earth in return for his benefactions. 'They think piety should earn interest, and of course piety does earn high interest, as long as one is content' (1 Tim. 6.5–6). The rich are to use their riches for the benefit of others, so acquiring a treasure which will form a good foundation for the future (6.19). The wrong attitude to riches is probably also reflected in the discussion of women's dress at worship. It has been suggested that in the communities behind the Pastorals there may have been a power struggle between those bearing the apostolic tradition and the rich who patronised the community. Yet it is householders, which implies well-to-do Christians, who are to be bishops and deacons, provided they have the right character, and are properly appointed by Paul's heirs with the proper commitment to the tradition.[31]

The difficulties in unearthing the nature of the false teachers stimulated the proposal that they are 'unreal'. They are typical heretics, rather than actual opponents. 'Judaism, legalism, mythology, and gnosis are lumped together in a way that suggests rather that the author was concerned to omit no heresy he had heard of than that he wished, or was able, to analyse, sub-divide and classify.'[32] My own view would be that it is unlikely these letters are without situation, and that the problems in the churches must have been real enough to have provoked the writing of these letters. But it is a fact of experience that church communities often struggle with a variety of issues which may or may not overlap. The Acts of Paul and Thecla appears to be anti-gnostic and as opposed as these letters to an over-realised eschatology; yet it clearly evidences other tendencies against which these letters seem to be ranged. The important advance is that scholars are no longer concen-

---

[31] Reggie M. Kidd, *Wealth and Beneficence in the Pastoral Epistles: A 'Bourgeois' Form of Early Christianity?*, SBL Dissertation Series 122 (Atlanta, GA, 1990); he develops a proposal of L. W. Countryman, *The Rich Christian in the Church of the Early Empire: Contradictions and Accommodations* (New York and Toronto, 1980). See further chapter 2.

[32] C. K. Barrett, 'Pauline Controversies in the Post-Pauline Period', *NTS* 20.3 (1974), 229–45 (240).

trating simply on questions of faith and order, but recognising that social factors and ethical questions are as important for any attempt to discern the background of these epistles. The biggest issue, however, may have been the proper interpretation of Paul's legacy.

CULTURAL CONTEXT

The Christian communities for which these epistles were intended are certainly to be located in a Hellenistic urban setting. Far more than in the authentic Paulines the vocabulary and allusions betray the assumptions of such a world. There are more traces of literary culture, such as the proverb about Cretans being liars, or the tag concerning love of money being the root of evils, for which many parallels can be supplied from contemporary literature.[33] The ethical codes follow patterns and use vocabulary which can again be dramatically paralleled in other Hellenistic texts, as we shall see.[34]

We are not in the presence of high literary culture, but we are in a social setting where elitist norms and values have filtered down. The language in which 'sound' (i.e. healthy) teaching is recommended and the minds of the opponents described as diseased, defiled and corrupt, their motives blackened and their hearers belittled has been compared with the standard claims and counter-claims of Cynic philosophers and public reaction to them: the original recipients of these letters were expected to recognise a 'type'.[35] The orthodox teacher, by contrast, is characterised as one who preaches to benefit others and to promote social stability, a picture which 'is in

---

[33] Dibelius–Conzelmann provide examples in the Hermeneia Commentary, p. 85.

[34] See chapter 2 below, pp. 31–3.

[35] See Abraham J. Malherbe, 'Medical Imagery in the Pastoral Epistles', originally published in *Texts and Testaments: Critical Essays on the Bible and Early Christian Fathers*, ed. W. E. March (San Antonio, TX, 1980), reprinted as chapter 8 of *Paul and the Popular Philosophers* (Minneapolis, 1989), pp. 121-36. For further delineation of the Cynic type, see also his article '"Gentle as a Nurse": The Cynic Background to 1 Thessalonians 2', originally published in *Novum Testamentum* 12 (1970) and republished as chapter 3 of *Paul and the Popular Philosophers*.

harmony with the overall tendency of the Pastoral Epistles to present Christianity as a responsible part of society'.[36]

On the other hand, these letters are pervaded by a religious culture that must stem from Hellenistic Judaism. The Jewish scriptures are honoured, though perhaps not well known (most actual quotations have been culled from the authentic Paulines); blessings and confessions in language that seems to sound the tones of Hellenistic Jewish synagogues punctuate the letters. A monotheism which evokes an exclusive worship and loyalty rather than theoretically undergirding the kind of philosophical syncretism that was widespread in the Hellenistic world is expressed in such passages, and, as we shall see, the organisational structures of the community may well reflect the norms of the contemporary synagogue in the Jewish Diaspora, where synagogues, like churches, were often located in houses. The piety practised is given the Hellenistic word *eusebeia*, a word not used by Paul, and indicative of this world of Hellenised Judaism. It has been well suggested that it represents the equivalent of the biblical phrase 'the fear of the Lord', a faith reflected in appropriate practice and lifestyle.[37]

Probably the people gathered in the church communities of the Pastorals were Gentiles not Jews, and the Jewish elements of their culture were mediated to them through the Christian tradition. Yet they are clearly in certain respects marginalised from their parent-culture, and this perhaps explains the overriding need not to draw attention to their peculiarities, and to avoid charges of subversive activities as far as humanly possible. But this is not the whole story: for true believers are prepared to face persecution, and the affirmation of a properly ordered lifestyle is given theological grounding. These Christians are seeking righteousness and dignity, and a good reputation, doubtless because they are convinced their tradition has imparted to them the true religion and the right way of life. Their culture is ambivalent, their social status inconsistent, but their conviction sure. The false teachers undermine their

---

[36] Malherbe, 'Medical Imagery', pp. 121–36 (p. 136).
[37] Towner, *The Goal of our Instruction*, pp. 147–54.

standing and challenge their ambiguous conformity. Is it surprising they present a very deep threat?

PURPOSE, DATE, AUTHOR

Theology is earthed in a context. The theology made explicit in the Pastorals relates to the problems the recipient communities are facing, for the purpose of the letters is to address those problems.

The author sees that the answer to these problems is to ensure that the communities are properly ordered and that suitable leaders are appointed whose authority will be obeyed. So the purpose of 1 Timothy and Titus is to provide guidance about church organisation, and the appropriate Christian lifestyle. This is done through adaptation of the household code to the household of God. The household code format, a kind of convention in moral discourse, had already been Christianised within the Pauline tradition and used for codifying ethical norms (Colossians, Ephesians); now further development produces the earliest 'church order'. However, 2 Timothy is rather different in character, presenting Paul as a kind of ideal convert and martyr, while encouraging people to avoid the false teachers. Radical opposition to the authorities is inappropriate, but people should not be ashamed of those imprisoned for their faith, or avoid taking their share of hardship and persecution. Its purpose would seem to be both paraenetic, Paul's life being exemplary, and also confirmatory, providing Paul's authoritative seal on the tradition claimed by these letters.

All written documents in the ancient world were recorded speech, and they were all audience-orientated in the sense that their principal purpose was to persuade the audience.[38] 'Proof' or conviction (*pistis* = 'faith') arose from the interplay of the *logos*, the argument or content, the *ēthos* of the speaker, the authority accorded by character, habit, manner of life, etc.,

---

[38] James L. Kinneavy, *Greek Rhetorical Origins of Christian Faith: An Inquiry* (Oxford, 1987), builds on standard rhetorical scholarship such as George Kennedy, *The Art of Rhetoric in the Roman World* (Princeton, 1972).

and the *pathos*, the response or feeling, generated in the audience. A letter was believed to make an absent person present.[39] Paul is absent, probably the hero-founder of the community or communities for which these epistles were intended. A new situation of crisis has arisen. Paul's authoritative word is needed. The tradition provides it. All that is needed is the right medium to make the absent Paul present. The discovery of more letters from Paul the letter-writer could hardly be unexpected. The compiler of the Acts of Paul found a Third Epistle to the Corinthians. But where that came from who knows?

Nor can we tell where the Pastorals came from. They emerge into the tradition during the second century. Polycarp and Theophilus seem to know them. Irenaeus accepts them as scriptural. Unlike the Acts of Paul they succeed in establishing themselves as authentic. Certainly they transmitted the Pauline tradition to the later church. But as to their origin, we seem to have to remain agnostic.[40] It is a good guess that they derive from Pauline churches in Asia Minor, and that they were composed in the late first century; but in all honesty, that is only a guess. Like Luke–Acts, they appropriate Paul for what would become the Christian 'mainstream', salvaging and developing what has been called the 'good Paul legend' in the face of the 'bad Paul legends' claimed by rival groups of a gnostic or extreme ascetic kind.[41]

---

[39] W. G. Doty, *Letters in Primitive Christianity* (Philadelphia, 1973).

[40] There has, of course, been a long debate about Pauline authorship. It was seriously challenged by P. N. Harrison, *The Problem of the Pastoral Epistles* (Oxford, 1921). J. N. D. Kelly defended Pauline authorship in the Black's Commentary, and conservatives have continued to argue against pseudonymity. The issues will be discussed further in the last chapter, but the consensus of New Testament historical scholarship is against authenticity.

[41] Barrett, 'Pauline Controversies'.

CHAPTER 2

Theology and ethics

There are some theological statements in the Pastoral epistles, but there is little theological argument, and the most obvious feature of these letters is that they are largely given over to ethical teaching. The question that this raises is the extent to which theology is merely incidental to the ethical interest of these epistles. It is important not to impose a framework on the texts we are examining, so we begin by considering their primary ethical content and asking how this interacts with, moulds or reflects their theology.

In the Greco-Roman environment, ethics was a branch of philosophy, and so might theology be, but there was usually little perceived connection between the two. In Jewish tradition, however, ethics and theology were inseparable: for the way of life set forth in Torah, revealed by God, constituted Jewish ethics.[1] To what extent did the Pastorals inherit that Jewish perspective? Or has ethics lost its theological foundation and become 'autonomous'?[2] Is it true that these epistles continue 'the movement ... away from the Pauline theological-

---

[1] Philosophy was divided by Stoics into logic, physics and ethics. In so far as the nature of the gods was a philosophical topic (e.g. Cicero, *The Nature of the Gods*, ET Penguin Classics (Harmondsworth, 1972)), it belonged to physics or metaphysics. Some, such as the Stoics, provided a theoretical base for ethics from physics, but not all did so, e.g. the Cynics. See discussion and references in Lewis R. Donelson, *Pseudepigraphy and Ethical Argument in the Pastoral Epistles*, Hermeneutische Untersuchungen zur Theologie (Tübingen, 1986), pp. 154ff. Morality had never been integral to Greco-Roman religion as it was for Jews. For a useful introduction to religion in the Hellenistic period, see Luther H. Martin, *Hellenistic Religions* (Oxford, 1987).
[2] As suggested of the Pastorals by J. L. Houlden, *Ethics and the New Testament* (Harmondsworth, 1973; republished Oxford, 1975).

eschatological grounding of ethics towards an unreflected ethics that is indistinguishable from good citizenship'?[3]

One charge brought against the Pastorals is that their 'bourgeois' ethics and social conformity value respectability rather than holiness. That would be another way of characterising a perceived drift away from a theological view of ethics, away from the assumption that the will of God is the source and ground of human conduct. Many have also attributed to the Pastorals a loss of the Pauline doctrine of grace and a turning to works-righteousness, which might again encourage a tendency to divorce ethics and faith, allowing less integration of theology and ethics, a slipping towards the divorce in Hellenistic philosophy. These issues provide the agenda for our enquiry in this chapter. We will begin with the question concerning the attitude to the Jewish law found in these texts.

THE JEWISH LAW

The people who taught a different doctrine apparently wanted to be *nomodidaskaloi*, teachers of the law. The question of law was therefore raised by the false teachers, and it provides our first insight into the theological tradition of these epistles.

'We know that the law is good', affirms **1 Timothy 1.8**. Many scholars have immediately reacted with suspicion, given Paul's repudiation of the law in Galatians and Romans. But Rom. 7.12 has affirmed that 'the law is holy and the commandment is holy and just and good'. In fact it is the subsequent comments that sound unlike Paul, though they are Pauline in the sense that the law is no longer applicable to Christians. As the REB puts it, we know the law is good, 'provided we treat it as law', a good rendering of the literal words, 'if we use it lawfully'. For this text suggests that it does apply to sinners and criminals, though not to 'good citizens' (REB). To a righteous person law is irrelevant, but not to 'lawless and unruly people, the impious and sinful, the irreligious and worldly, parricides

---

[3] Jack T. Sanders, *Ethics in the New Testament* (London, 1975), p. 88.

and matricides, murderers and fornicators, perverts, kidnappers, liars, perjurers'.

The list is at first sight rather curious, including as it does both the horror crimes of classical mythology, parricide and matricide, and moral sensitivities about sexual perversion which must derive from the Jewish background given the Greek tendency to celebrate homosexual love. A closer look situates this list in the Hellenistic-Jewish bridge-culture we have posited: on the one hand philosophers regularly listed sacrilege or temple-spoiling, murder, parricide and matricide as (admittedly extreme!) examples of sins,[4] on the other hand, the list implies the Decalogue, the 'impious and sinful' being those who break the first commandments concerning God's worship and name, the 'irreligious and worldly' representing those who break the Sabbath and religious commandments, 'parricides and matricides' typifying failure to honour father and mother, and the rest following the order of the remaining Ten Commandments against murder, adultery, etc.[5]

But the point is pretty clear. Law is taken to operate as in any society, being designed to regulate anti-social behaviour – the good citizen is unlikely to be affected by the legal system. It is important to realise that the Jewish law, like any other code of law, originated as the law of a state, that the Greco-Roman world was fascinated by law and by the ancient lawgivers who had founded and legislated for important ancient cities, such as Athens and Rome. Moses was regarded as the law-giver of the Jews,[6] and in Greek, the Torah (which meant

---

[4] For detailed references, consult Dibelius–Conzelmann.

[5] See further Kelly and Dibelius–Conzelmann.

[6] The general observations in this paragraph undergird the argument of Josephus in his apologetic work *Contra Apionem* 2.154–6, where, referring to proverbial founders and law-givers of cities such as Athens and others, he maintains that Moses is the most ancient law-giver: 'Compared with him, your Lycurgus and Solon and Seleucus, who gave the Locrians their laws, and all who have been held in high esteem by the Greeks, appear to have been born yesterday. Why, the very word 'law' (*nomos*) was unknown in ancient Greece ... On the other hand, our legislator, who lived in remotest antiquity ... proved himself the people's best guide and counsellor; after framing a code to embrace the whole conduct of their life, [he] induced them to accept it, and secured on the firmest footing its observance for all time.' This argument can be paralleled in other Hellenistic Jewish authors. See Arthur J. Droge, *Homer or Moses?*, Hermeneutische Untersuchungen zur Theologie (Tübingen, 1989).

something like 'revelatory teaching') became *nomos*, custom or law. It was therefore quite understandable that Christian converts should equate Jewish law with the civil and criminal law of a state.

But of course that was not the kind of issue at stake when Paul debated the relevance of law to Christian converts. Obedience to certain customs such as circumcision, dietary laws and purity regulations had come to be the distinguishing marks of Jews faithful to the religious traditions of their people. The practice of Jewish customs which affected the everyday lifestyle of converts or proselytes, the adoption of the ethnic marks of a Jew, had been in Paul's time the issue with respect to law.[7] For the God-given law of the Jews was understood not merely to regulate socially acceptable behaviour, but to provide guidance on how life was to be lived. Of course there was no debate about the applicability of universally regarded moral precepts or legal dictates to Christians, whether Jews or Gentiles. There clearly was some tension about the adoption of Jewish sexual ethics (see 1 Thessalonians, 1 Corinthians), and here Paul had had no hesitation in requiring traditional Jewish standards from his Gentile converts. That is reflected in this list, as we have already noted. But the issue as debated by Paul is apparently long settled now. Law is irrelevant to the 'righteous one' since such a person will keep it all anyway just by being a good citizen and a loyal Christian.

If commentators are right to discern the Decalogue behind the list, then an important step is being taken for the future of Christianity. Embryonically we have the recognition of the distinction between the cultic and the moral law which would come to characterise Christian appropriation of the 'old covenant'. The moral law, especially as enshrined in the Decalogue, would be treated as still in force. The Jewish scriptures would continue to be regarded as God's Word, and God's Word was to be obeyed. In other words, the discussion implies the assumption, which I shall argue underlies the whole of these

---

[7] See discussion in J. D. G. Dunn, *The Theology of Galatians* (Cambridge, 1993).

letters, that *theology and ethics are inseparable*. The divine will shaped the way of life which was pure and acceptable. Ethics could not be a mere matter of habit or preference or even conforming to society's laws. The climax of the list of those for whom the law does apply is 'all whose behaviour flouts the sound teaching which conforms with the gospel entrusted to me, the gospel which tells of the glory of the ever-blessed God' (1 Tim. 1.8). Somehow the gospel provides teaching which has to be followed. If this initial discussion focusses on law as a hedge against what does not conform, these letters will soon become primarily interested in the kind of ethics required by the gospel.

THE PERFORMANCE OF GOOD WORKS

These letters encourage Christian readers to 'good works'. Women and widows are particularly expected to perform 'good works' (1 Tim. 2.10; 5.10), but so are the rich (1 Tim. 6.18). Just as bad deeds will out, so will good deeds (1 Tim. 5.25). The vessel that is cleansed from wickedness is useful to the master and fit for every good work (2 Tim. 2.21), and the 'man of God' like Timothy is fit for every good work (2 Tim. 3.17). 'Titus' is to set an example of good works (Titus 2.7). But the unfaithful who profess to know God but deny it by their actions are disobedient and unfit for any good work (Titus 1.16). The saving action of Christ set Christians free from wickedness to make a people for himself, eager for good works (Titus 2.14). So everyone is to be reminded to be ready for good works (Titus 3.14). The purpose of insisting on the teaching of the gospel is to ensure that those who have come to faith may have the intention of excelling in good works (Titus 3.8, reinforced in Titus 3.14). In the light of Paul's criticism of works in Romans (e.g. 3.20–4.6), this has often been treated as an un-Pauline stress.

However, there are allusions to Paul's argument that salvation depends on prior rescue from sin and wickedness which God's grace alone could effect, and cannot be a matter of reward for works of righteousness:

He is the one who saved us and called us with a holy calling, not according to our works but according to the divine purpose and grace, granted to us in Christ Jesus before ancient times, and revealed now through the appearance of our Saviour Jesus Christ. (2 Tim. 1.9ff.)

But when the kindness and love of our Saviour God dawned upon the world, then, he saved us, not through works of righteousness we had done, but according to the divine mercy, through the bath of rebirth and the renewal of the Holy Spirit, which was poured out richly upon us through Jesus Christ our Saviour, so that, justified by his grace, we might in hope become heirs to eternal life. That is a saying you may trust. (Titus 3.4–8a)

That last phrase (*pistos ho logos* = (lit.) 'faithful is the saying') is fairly frequent in these letters, and perhaps draws attention to particular 'slogans' of the tradition. But it is unclear whether in the context and structure of the text, it is retrospective, or prospective. Perhaps settling that question is not so necessary after all; for what is interesting is that the succeeding statement is the one urging insistence on these points precisely to ensure that those who have come to faith devote themselves to good works. These texts see no contradiction between 'good works' and the Pauline tradition that salvation is by the grace and generosity of God. Salvation by grace not works makes possible the practice of good works; without proper belief, a person is disqualified from good works (Titus 1.16), while with proper belief, a godly life may be lived, and that will be expressed in eagerness for good works.

How far is this a proper interpretation of Paul's position? It would seem to me to be a fair if simplified representation of exactly what Paul thought. For too long, Pauline scholarship was shaped by the assumption that Paul was negative towards the law and towards works,[8] simply because of his doctrine of justification not by works but by grace through faith. In Romans Paul quite explicitly rejects the antinomian logic: he claims to uphold the law (Rom. 3.31), he refuses to countenance the idea that 'the more sin the more grace' (Rom. 6.1),

---

[8] See discussion of 'not works of the law' in Dunn, *Galatians*.

insisting that 'sin shall be no longer your master, for you are no longer under law but under grace' (Rom. 6.14), and he speaks of the 'just commandment of the law' finding 'fulfilment in us, whose conduct is no longer controlled by the old nature, but by the Spirit' (Romans 8.4). Furthermore, in the Corinthian correspondence, 'work' is what Christian apostles do (1 Cor. 3.13,14,15; 9.1; 16.10), and the Corinthians are urged to work for the Lord, and to 'overflow' with 'every good work' (1 Cor. 15.58, 2 Cor. 9.8); even in Galatians (6.4) all are to examine their own work, and in Romans Paul suggests that the government holds no terror for 'good work' (13.3), while 2.1–16 depends on the view that everyone will be judged or rewarded for their 'works'. The Pastorals spell out Paul's conception that good practice is to be expected of the converted, even if the grace of God, not human righteousness, effects salvation.

The exact meaning of Paul's argument has been the subject of much debate recently as a result of the work of E. P. Sanders.[9] He challenged the post-Reformation reading of Paul's justification doctrine, especially what had become the standard opposition between faith and works. Sanders has insisted that while the law was not an 'entry qualification' for Gentiles, nevertheless the new covenant community had its moral and ethical requirements. The Pastorals offer some confirmation of his view, demonstrating that something like his reading was indeed the understanding of Paul which passed to the mainstream church. This is not the place to be diverted into reviewing the debate about Paul's own position. We simply note that many of the standard comments about the Pastorals' shift of perspective on the issue of faith and works need revision in the light of the new perspective on Paul that has been emerging.

---

[9] E. P. Sanders, *Paul and Palestinian Judaism* (London, 1977); *Paul, the Law and the Jewish People* (Philadelphia, 1983); *Paul,* Past Masters series (Oxford, 1990). Chief participants in the debate with Sanders have been H. Räisänen and J. D. G. Dunn, with Hans Hübner representing the more traditional Protestant view. Access to the most important contributions can be found by reference to the relevant chapters of James D. G. Dunn, *Jesus, Paul and the Law* (London, 1990), together with his notes and references.

The Pastorals proclaim Paul's gospel of grace, but insist that the outcome of the gospel is a change in behaviour:

> For the saving grace of God has appeared for all humankind; and by it we are trained to refuse ungodliness and worldly desires, and to live a life of self-control, righteousness and piety in the present age, looking forward to the blessed hope and the glorious appearing of the great God and our Saviour Jesus Christ. He it is who gave himself for us, to set us free from all wickedness and to purify for himself a chosen people, eager to do good. (Titus 2.11–14)

The theological statements in this passage will be discussed in the next chapter. The point here is the evident dependence of doing good and renouncing sinful ways upon the gracious saving activity of God. Good works result from salvation, which comes from God the Saviour. What good works did the Pastorals have in mind? Those good works which result from salvation are certainly the practice of charity and what we might call welfare support (1 Tim. 6.17–19, where the rich are in view, and this is also implied by the 1 Timothy references to women's good works). But probably they also embrace all the qualities and moral standards approved in these letters. The whole lifestyle is grounded in God's activity and will. The ethics of the Pastorals are fundamentally theological.

THE ETHICAL TEACHING – ITS SHAPE, CONTENT AND CHARACTER

Ethics, deriving from the Greek *ēthos*, refers to the whole complex of habits, customs and lifestyle which make up a person's character. Character was understood to be constituted by roles and duties in the ancient world – our conceptions of person have been profoundly changed by the introspective individualism and psychologising of the modern world.[10] Typical ethical discourses in popular philosophical teaching[11]

---

10 Bruce Malina, *The New Testament World: Insights from Cultural Anthropology* (London, 1983). The case is perhaps a little overstated, but see further below, chapter 4.
11 See David C. Verner's review of the *Haustafel schēma/topos* in *The Household of God: The Social World of the Pastoral Epistles*, SBL Dissertation Series 71 (Chico, CA, 1983), pp. 84ff. Drawing on the earlier work of D. L. Balch, *Let Wives be Submissive: The*

focussed on the appropriate qualities of character required for people in certain positions, and on the conduct of particular relationships, such as master/slave, parent/child, husband/ wife, ruler/ruled, rich/poor.

So one of the most fascinating set of parallels to the material in the Pastorals is the text[12] outlining the qualities of the good general reproduced as an Appendix to the Dibelius– Conzelmann commentary. The first paragraph lists the qualities expected, the succeeding paragraphs contain commentary on each. The good general is to be temperate, self-restrained, vigilant, frugal, hardened to labour, alert, free from avarice, neither too young nor too old, a father of children, a ready speaker and a man with a good reputation. Many of these Greek adjectives are exactly paralleled in the descriptions of the *episkopos* in 1 Timothy 3 and Titus 1: *sōphrōn*, 'temperate', *enkratēs*, 'self-restrained', *aphilarguros*, 'free from avarice'; and other qualities are very similar, such as having a good reputation, being a father, being not too old or young and being a good teacher. Thus the Pastorals fit into common Hellenistic discourse.

But much of such discourse was already adapted to Christian use in the Pauline tradition. The lists of duties found in Colossians and Ephesians and known as household codes are of particular interest here, since the Pastorals seem almost to take them over and adapt them to discussion of duties within the household of God.

There has been extended scholarly discussion about the form of household codes, and the extent to which a distinguishable *topos* or *schēma* can be traced back either to Stoic duty codes, or the discussions of household management found in Aristotle's *Politics* and similar philosophical texts.[13] What is incontrovertibly evident is that behind the Pauline codes are traditions of *paraenesis* in Hellenistic philosophical discourse which were

---

Domestic Code in I Peter (Chico, CA, 1981), he notes in particular the beginning of Aristotle's *Politics*, as well as Dionysius of Halicarnassus, Epictetus, Philo, etc.

[12] Onosander, *De Imperatoris Officio* 1.

[13] Verner, *The Household of God*, has an extended discussion of scholarly investigation since Dibelius.

flexibly shaped according to conventional patterns and concerned to map out appropriately the required character and relations between those persons who exercised different functions within the state or the household. It is also pretty clear that such codes form the basis of the ethical teaching of the Pastorals, so for convenience I shall continue to describe them as household codes. Dibelius wanted to see certain core passages, notably Titus 2, as being household codes proper giving instructions to members of the family, including slaves; but he thought these were amalgamated with primitive church orders, such as are found in the *Didachē*. It would seem more plausible to suggest that church orders themselves emerged from Christian adaptation of something like household codes.

The important point here is that the Pastorals pick up familiar ethical genres and adapt them to spelling out the Christian way of life, working through the typical roles within the household of God. Precisely how this is done in relation to church order will be examined in chapter 5. Suffice it to emphasise here that it is the qualities of character rather than the functions of various people in God's household which are delineated, as in the case of the *episkopos* already examined.

The discourse, then, is typically Hellenistic. But does this make it culturally accommodating, conservative and conformist, or 'bourgeois'? Such an estimate has been current since Dibelius, who saw the Pastorals as reflecting a time when Christians were settling down in the world, and their ethic as encouraging good citizenship. This view has been subject to careful examination by Reggie M. Kidd.[14] By surveying work on ancient society and the position of Christians within it, he is able to offer an important warning against projecting any kind of modern 'middle class' into analysis of the social world of antiquity. Christians did not belong to the small elite orders of Roman imperial society, but some did belong to local elites. The urban societies in which Christianity flourished had within them an 'acute stratification', and a developed sense of reciprocity in relations between different social strata. Early

---

[14] Kidd, *Wealth and Beneficence.*

Christian literature and the Pastorals in particular reflect expectations arising from the natural dominance of the well-to-do, on whom an association like the church depended for patronage, for a household within which to meet, for leadership, finance and benefactions.

Demonstrating the value-systems of the ancient world with respect to the use of wealth, such as the reciprocal relationship of 'honour' (*timē*) and benefit derived from generosity to the municipality, or the client in need of support, Kidd draws out important ways in which the Pastorals, while reflecting those values, subject them to criticism. Concentrating on the passage relating to rich Christians (1 Tim. 6.6–10, 17–19), he notes that the acquisition and proper use of wealth was another feature of traditional ethical *paraenesis*, and that some features of the Pastorals' teaching are conventional: the precariousness of wealth, the assumption that the power of wealth lies in benefiting others and 'being rich in good deeds', that the good and noble thing to do was to be a benefactor – these would be familiar sentiments to wealthy residents of Greco-Roman cities. (It is worth noting that the Pastorals, when they speak of 'good works', often use the Greek forms of *kalon ergon* rather than Paul's *ergon agathon*, and this reflects the background in beneficence and patronage noted here.)

But 'the assumption that wealth is an index of moral worth is dismissed out of hand' (p. 157). Christian benefactors are not to expect earthly glory, and the typical language of making 'friends' through generosity is entirely missing. Reward belongs to another age and comes from God. Status and honour in the church comes from other sources, and the Christian value-system exalts the lowly. So, although it reflects Greco-Roman values, we must also reassert that this ethical material is Christianised and brought into a fundamentally theological frame.

The theological focus is evident from the beginning. 1 Timothy speaks first of behaviour at prayer, the principal activity of the assembled household of God. The ethics of prayer begin at **1 Timothy 2.1**. Like Jews, Christians are to offer prayers for the constituted rulers and authorities, expecting in return permission to pursue their religion unmolested. The theological undergirding of this is the belief that there is only one God, as we shall see in the next chapter. Moving to verse 8, we notice a differentiation between men and women. Men have the duty of saying the prayers, and they must do this with the proper stance and the proper attitude: 'lifting up holy hands, without anger or argument' is perhaps reminiscent of the drift of certain striking sayings in the Sermon on the Mount (e.g. Matt. 5.23–4; 6.7–15). Almost certainly the duty of men to pray and women to listen derives from synagogue practice, though it is not easy to determine the date at which men and women were seated separately.[15] It is evident, however, that the distinct religious roles of men and women were part of the stuff of Jewish tradition. As in traditional Middle Eastern societies to this day,[16] there was a clear distinction between the public and private sphere, and women belonged to the latter. The quorum in the synagogue consisted of males; women were freed of the male religious obligations in order to fulfil their domestic duties, which were themselves religious and ritualistic in certain respects.

This traditional separation of the worlds of men and women was probably somewhat threatened by the mores of the Hellenistic world, and already Paul had attempted to regulate things according to his idea of what was proper (1 Cor. 14.33–5). The fact that the private sphere of the household was the locus of the public meeting of the congregation, and that in certain ways the Christians saw themselves as God's family in the household of God, no doubt helped to blur the edges.

---

15 E. Schürer, *The History of the Jewish People in the Age of Jesus Christ*, new edition edited by Geza Vermes, Fergus Millar and Matthew Black (Edinburgh, 1979), vol. II, pp. 447–8, assumes the segregation of the sexes. Bernadette J. Brooten, *Women Leaders in the Ancient Synagogue* (Chico, CA, 1982), argued for an active role for women in ancient synagogues from inscriptional evidence, and this is followed by Paul Trebilco, *Jewish Communities in Asia Minor*, SNTS Monograph Series 69 (Cambridge, 1991). This has been contested, however, on the grounds that Mishnaic culture excludes women from the public domain. See James Tunstead Burtchaell, *From Synagogue to Church: Public Services and Offices in the Earliest Christian Communities* (Cambridge, 1992), pp. 244–5 with notes.
16 Susan Starr Sered, *Women as Ritual Experts: The Religious Lives of Elderly Jewish Women in Jerusalem* (Oxford, 1992).

If women appeared in the 'public' world, they were to be modestly dressed, though the emphasis here is not simply on decorum; there is an implied criticism of rich display, and an emphasis on adornment in 'good works' rather than gold and pearls which is no doubt linked with the emphasis elsewhere on simplicity of life and the proper use of riches (1 Tim. 6.17–19). Nevertheless it is clear that in the context of the public congregation women were not to draw attention to themselves. Furthermore, even though it is not impossible that some women were to give instruction in the women's quarters (Titus 2.4),[17] in the public gathering they were not to teach or dictate to the men, but keep quiet. A scriptural justification is offered for this – with serious consequences for Christian projection of the blame for sin onto Eve and all women with her. At this point, however, we need to see the importance of this in the context of the author and his readers.

As noted in the previous chapter, it may well be the case that the disruption to households caused by radical ascetic teaching lies in the background of the Pastorals. Though in some ways clearly Gentile and removed from the Jewish context, the Pastorals seem to call upon Jewish religious and social mores to counter disorder in the community (as indeed Paul did in Corinth). There is much in these epistles which seeks to regulate the place and behaviour of celibate women, and counter excesses. The maintenance of the traditional differentiation of public and domestic spheres, and of the 'proper' roles of women is fundamental to this. So is the normality of childbearing – is not barrenness the most serious reproach to a woman in the Jewish scriptures, as the cases of Sarah and Hannah indicate? Although that point is not explicitly made, the suggestion that 'she will be saved by child-bearing' (1 Tim. 2.15) may be deeply shaped by the contrary view that women were to be saved by devotion to Christ and celibate rejection of traditional roles such as is found in the Apocryphal Acts.

---

[17] That women should minister to women, and therefore the bishop should appoint deaconesses for the purpose, is clear in the *Didascalia Apostolorum*, chapter xvi. This document prohibits women from teaching, but the ministry of women to women

In the face of the false teaching, an ethic is being given theological grounding by drawing upon scripture and on precedents offered by Paul himself in his epistles. It is worth noting that child-bearing is only effective for salvation if accompanied by faith, love and holiness with modesty (1 Tim. 2.15). These are qualities deeply rooted in the Christian tradition, and in the Pauline material grounded in Christological or theological ideas, such as the body being a temple of the Holy Spirit (1 Cor. 6.19). A specific practical understanding of what is implied for women by the classic Christian virtues is being offered in the face of a rival interpretation.

So the whole section 1 Tim. 2.1–15 is concerned with religious duties – even the remarks on women's dress – for the point is to regulate public prayer in the proper way, but already we can sense that there is no aspect of life which is not a 'religious duty'. The text confirms this by next characterising the lifestyle and *ēthos* of those with specific duties in the household of God, the head-steward and the servants or waiters (*episkopos* and *diakonoi*). Later the widows and the senior members of the community are likewise told how to behave. Who these various people may have been in terms of developing church offices will be considered later. What concerns us immediately is the kind of *ēthos* enjoined on these people.

And it is soon evident that no matter how Hellenistic the characterisation looks, the classic Christian virtues we have just noted in relation to women's *ēthos* recur throughout these three letters – indeed the fact that the same Christian qualities are expected of both men and women is striking. Faith, love and fortitude repeatedly return (Titus 2.2, cf. 1 Tim. 1.5,14; 4.12; 6.2,11; 2 Tim. 2.22; 3.10), and 'the spirit God gave us is no cowardly spirit, but one of power, love and self-discipline' (2 Tim. 1.7); love appears to have its source in God's grace, in Jesus Christ or the Holy Spirit (cf. Titus 2.11ff.; 3.5–8). Features in the lists of virtues give them a characteristically Jewish or Christian flavour, such as the virtue of hospitality (1

---

includes some teaching. There are good reasons for seeing here a natural development from the instructions in the Pastoral epistles.

Tim. 3.2; Titus 1.8), or the emphasis on lack of deceit and
double-talk reminiscent of the Psalms, or the call to a strict
marital ethic, to purity and holiness, qualities which have
cultic rather than moral roots, here embodied in the dedicated
life to which God calls his servants (2 Tim. 1.9). These office-
holders are to be not only trustworthy but also just and devout.
Behaviour is the manifestation of qualities grounded in specific
Christian and scriptural virtues. Traditional the *paraenesis* may
be in form and content, but the ethics are deeply integrated
with the theological outlook of the community. Indeed the
requisite purity only issues from proper belief (Titus 1.15).

All this is well exemplified by the description of the 'man of
God', the church leader represented by 'Timothy' (1 Tim.
6.11ff.): the man of God is to pursue justice, piety, integrity,
love, fortitude and gentleness, to run the great race of faith and
take hold of eternal life. It was to this that the man of God is
called, and it requires making confession before witnesses, as
Christ did before Pilate. Throughout these epistles, ethical
argument utilises exemplary paradigms; Christ and Paul and
Timothy figure (e.g. 1 Tim. 1.16 (and context), 4.12ff.; 6.11ff.;
2 Tim. 1.13; 2.8–10; 3.10–12; Titus 3.3ff.).

In fact, in an interesting analysis of the forms of argument
found in the Pastorals, Lewis Donelson[18] has argued not only
that there are such Christian paradigms undergirding the
logic, but that assumptions about God and salvation constitute
the underlying premises of identifiable 'enthymemes' or rhetorical deductions. My interest here is not so much in the
underlying structure of argument, but the theological
grounding, which is striking. Specific ethical issues, such as the
appropriateness of extreme asceticism, or the proper use of
riches, are treated to arguments with a theological starting-
point: (1) Everything God created is good; God created food to
be enjoyed with thanksgiving; nothing is to be rejected, provided it is accepted with thanksgiving, for it is then made holy
by God's Word and prayer (1 Tim. 4.3–5). (2) God richly
provides all things for us to enjoy; we brought nothing into the

---

[18] Donelson, *Pseudepigraphy and Ethical Argument*, chapter 2.

world and will take nothing out; we should be content if we have food and clothing; if we are rich, we should be rich in well-doing and giving generously (1 Tim. 6.7–10, 17–19).

Thus, for all the parallels and suggested dependencies, the ethical teaching offered in these epistles would only carry conviction in a community that shared the fundamental theological presuppositions which undergird the discourse. We noted that the programming of Christian ethics in these letters began with appropriate behaviour in prayer (1 Tim. 2.1ff.). For these texts, the *ēthos* of the Christian way of life begins with prayer. The character expressed in prayer is that constantly reiterated in the 'codes': prayer is to be offered with pure intention and without anger or argument (1 Tim. 2.8) – in other words in single-mindedness, without deceit, in love and harmony; faith, love, holiness and modesty are the qualities not only of silent women (1 Tim. 2.15), but of community leaders. The good widow puts all her trust in God, as does the church leader, and her attendence at meetings for prayer and worship, day and night, is the grounding of that trust and hope (1 Tim. 5.5). It is all too easy to focus on the 'patriarchal' ethos of the codes, and miss the essentially religious and spiritual grounding of the practical advice given in order to express Christian values in a particular social context threatened by what was seen to be a dangerous rejection of the world and society as ordered by God.

THE CHRISTIAN IN THE WORLD

For good reason, as we have seen, these epistles encouraged a less than radical view of existing society and accepted the traditional hierarchical structures of the public and private worlds in which these Christians found themselves. What was needed in the context was a practical exposition of how Christian life was to be lived in the world. The adoption of the conventional Hellenistic shape of ethical teaching which focussed on the relationship of master and slave, husband and wife, father and child, ruler and subject inevitably tended to encourage conformity with well-established authority structures, but in any case, it was precisely that which was perceived as necessary in view of the immediate threat posed by contrary teachings, either of a too spiritual and other-worldly kind (gnostic) or of too radical and socially disruptive a kind (as in the Apocryphal Acts), or perhaps both.

Yet in their own way, those who produced and read these letters reveal themselves as deeply aware of their unconventionality and their marginalisation in relation to wider society. All the more reason, then, not to appear unnecessarily threatening to the established order!

Do not be ashamed of the witness of our Lord, nor of me a prisoner for his sake, but according to God's power accept your share of suffering for the sake of the gospel. (2 Tim. 1.8)

All of those who want to live a pious life in Jesus Christ, will be persecuted. (2 Tim. 3.12)

Run the great race of faith and take hold of eternal life, to which you were called, when you made your great confession before many witnesses. Now in the presence of God, who gives life to all things, and of Jesus Christ, who himself made that great confession before Pontius Pilate, I charge you to keep the commandment without fault or blame. (1 Tim. 6.12ff.)

The presence of such passages indicates that any view of these letters suggesting that Christians are settling down in the world and the theological-eschatological dimension is fading, is wide of the mark. That some kind of apocalyptic expectation is still alive will emerge in the following chapter.[19]

Two concerns are discernible. One is that those who suffer for their faith may be spurned by those who see Christianity as requiring 'a good reputation with the outside world' (1 Tim. 3.7): it was a disgrace to go to prison, to face condemnation. The other is to ensure that Christians are not apprehended for the wrong reasons.

Remind them to be submissive to rulers and authorities, and to obey them; to be ready for every good work; to slander no one, to avoid quarrels, and to show every gentleness to all people. (Titus 3.1–2)

---

[19] And see also Kidd, *Wealth and Beneficence*, chapter 4, 'Ethics and Eschatology in the Pastoral Epistles'.

The preference for social conformity appears not just in relation to the household but to the state. That the two spheres were interconnected had a background in conventional ethical teaching, for the household was held to mirror the state, and the proper ordering of households was seen as a vital element in maintaining law and order in society as a whole. The Pastorals reflect a fear of Christians being seen as socially disruptive for the wrong reasons, while needing to encourage the faithful to remain loyal to Christ under pressure. Their position in society is uncomfortably insecure, and they have to work out what it means for Christians to live in the world but be not of the world, to bear a brave witness if called to do so, but not besmirch the name of Christ by inviting persecution for criminal or immoral activities.

In fact the situation of **1 Peter** is much closer to the background of these epistles than has sometimes been recognised. It was clearly written against a background of persecution, and the readers are encouraged to find cause for joy in sufferings (1.6ff.). The suffering of Christ is both redemptive and exemplary (1.19ff.; 4.1–2, 13ff.). Yet it is important only to suffer for the name of Christ and not for wrong-doing – indeed we find here the same concern about people feeling it a disgrace to suffer (4.14–16). In this epistle too the proper characteristics of the various members of God's household (a phrase used in 4.17 to describe the church) are spelled out in the household code form, and the submission enjoined on those lower in the hierarchies includes obedience to the emperor and to the governors as his deputies (2.13ff.). The same virtues are encouraged, and the same stewardship of what God has provided. Servants and women are to submit to the present order, and younger people to older people. The note here that does not sound in the Pastorals is the sense of the Christian community, who once were 'not my people', becoming 'God's people' and inheriting the priestly responsibility for the world which once belonged to Israel.

And yet in a sense this is presupposed in the Pastorals also. Christians are encouraged to pray, like Jews in their synagogues, for sovereigns and all those in high office, offering on

their behalf petitions, intercessions, thanksgivings. This is justified on the ground that there is only one God. What is necessary is to exercise appropriate responsibility for the world, and
so to find ways of living responsibly in the world, despite its
transience. The eschatological dimension is more explicit in 1
Peter, but hardly absent in the Pastorals:

Know this: in the last days, there will be difficult times. (2 Tim. 3.1)

Before God, and before Christ Jesus who will judge the living and the
dead, I charge you solemnly by his epiphany and his kingdom,
proclaim the word. (2 Tim. 4.1–2)

And yet for all the similarities, the Pastorals seem to reflect a
further development towards the forms and attitudes reflected
in the Apostolic Fathers. 1 Peter does not bear the marks of
moving from the ethical teaching of a household code to a
primitive church order, as the Pastorals do. By the time we
reach Polycarp's *Letter to the Philippians* which is widely recognised to be remarkably close to the Pastorals, so much so that
von Campenhausen suggested Polycarp as the unknown
author of the Pastorals,[20] the household code has become
further diluted.[21] Like 1 Peter, the situation of Polycarp's letter
reminds us that the ethical teaching has to be set in a context of
actual or imminent persecution, for Polycarp refers to the
recent visit of Ignatius on his way to Rome to be thrown to the
wild beasts,[22] and the best-known fact about Polycarp himself
is that he died as a martyr in old age, the earliest extant
example of Martyr Acts being the account of his glorious
passing. There could be no compromise if asked to deny Christ
and say, 'Caesar is Lord.'

Against that background, we read his exhortation to the life
of holiness:

---

[20] Hans von Campenhausen, 'Polykarp von Smyrna und die Pastoralbriefe', in *Aus der
Frühezeit des Christentums* (Tübingen, 1963).

[21] See Verner, *The Household of God*.

[22] Ignatius' journey was around AD 110, and that gives an approximate dating for
Polycarp's letter. Some forty years later Polycarp was martyred in advanced old
age.

the first step must be to school our own selves into conformity with the divine commandments. After that we can go on to instruct our womenfolk in the traditions of the faith, and in love and purity; teaching them to show fondness and fidelity to their husbands, and a chaste and impartial affection for everyone else, and to bring up their children in the faith of God. (Polycarp, *Phil.* 4)[23]

He goes on to exhort widows to observe discretion as they practise the faith, to make constant intercessions for everyone, to avoid tale-bearing and tittle-tattle, and misconduct of every kind: 'They are to recognise they are an altar of God.' Further sections speak of the need for deacons to be beyond reproach and exhort younger men to purity, and the whole letter is punctuated with warnings about love of money: 'We know we brought nothing into this world and we can carry nothing out', he says echoing the Pastorals. The same values, virtues and characteristics as those enjoined in the Pastorals reappear.

Ignatius wrote to Polycarp on his journey, and while the similarities are less striking, we find him offering Polycarp advice as a church leader which has the same ring as the advice offered to 'Timothy' and 'Titus'. Slaves should aim to be better slaves for the glory of God, and not expect the church to purchase their freedom; women are to content themselves with their own husbands, but as in all these texts, husbands are also told to love and respect their wives.

If somebody is capable of spending all his days in chastity, in honour of the Lord's body, let him do so without any boasting. (Ignatius, *Polycarp* 5)[24]

Celibacy appears as a superior ideal in the minds of some, but there are reservations, and anyone intending to get married should get the approval of the bishop.

Also interesting are the similarities with **1 Clement.** This letter was written around AD 96 in response to disruption and dispute in the Corinthian church, and begins by characterising their former excellence and constancy in the faith:

[23] Translation from Penguin Classics volume *Early Christian Writings*, p. 120.
[24] *Ibid.*, p. 110.

Who ever failed to be impressed by your sober and selfless Christian piety, to tell of your generous spirit of hospitality, or to pay tribute to the wide range and soundness of your knowledge? It was your habit at all times to act without fear or favour, living by the laws of God and deferring with correctness to those who were set over you. Your elders were treated with the honour due to them; your young men were counselled to be soberly and seriously minded; your women folk were bidden to go about their duties in irreproachable devotion and purity of conscience, showing all proper affection for their husbands; they were taught to make obedience the rule of their lives, to manage their households decorously, and to be patterns of discretion in every way. (1 Clem. 1–2)[25]

All alike in the church are commended for their former humility, lack of self-assertion, and submission, accepting whatever Christ provided for the journey through life.

In the beauty of a pure and heavenly citizenship, whatever you did was done in the fear of God, and the statutes and judgments of the Lord were engraved on the tables of your hearts. (1 Clem. 2)

Not only does this suggest similar ideas about Christian lifestyle to those found in the Pastorals, but it also confirms that such ideas were rooted in a theological perspective. Christians had their citizenship in heaven; they were in one sense aliens from the world of Roman society. Yet in another sense since the social order in God's world ultimately had some kind of divine sanction, the order of this world was to be respected and upheld. This passage also shows how the notion of God's laws under the new covenant being written on the heart, a view dear to Paul (2 Cor. 3), undergirded the ethics of the emerging church.

Later in the epistle, positive exhortation reinforces the same set of values as we have found in the Pastorals:

let us be respectful to those who have been set over us, honour our elders, and train up our young people in the fear of God; let us set our womenfolk on the road to goodness, by teaching them to be examples of lovable purity, to display real sincerity in their submissiveness, to prove the self-restraint of their tongues by observing silence, and to

[25] *Ibid.*, p. 23.

bestow equal affection, with no favouritism and as becomes holiness, upon all God-fearing persons. (1 Clem. 21)[26]

and we find a very similar injunction to appropriate attitudes in prayer:

we must approach him in holiness of spirit, lifting up pure and undefiled hands to him in love for the gracious and compassionate Father who has chosen us to be his own. (1 Clem. 29)[27]

The Pastorals are clearly within the stream of those developments represented by the Apostolic Fathers. All these documents reveal in one way or another their links with the Pauline tradition; all stand outside the gnostic Pauline heritage, and all show a primary interest in ethics, in the gospel as the revelation of the right way of life. All display a similar moulding by the Hellenistic world which was the context in which the Christian life had to be lived. Yet the tradition they inherit makes their communities conscious of living as strangers in the world, being citizens of heaven, looking forward to the kingdom of God, belonging neither to the Jewish race nor to the culture and society of the Gentile world where they belonged in terms of their kith and kin. Before the second century was out, they would regard themselves as the 'third race'.[28] Their ethics are theological ethics, their God is the God of the universe, and their way of life is the divine will revealed in Christ and the scriptures, and potentially the universal way for all good citizens to follow. All that may not yet be entirely explicit in the Pastorals, but these letters certainly belong to that kind of developing Christian consciousness.

It does not seem helpful to characterise these attitudes as 'bourgeois', and the argument of this chapter has been that they are not appropriately described as offering an 'autonomous' or non-theological ethic, nor do they suggest a church settling down in the world. Underlying the teaching is a sense of alienation which itself makes it the more urgent to encourage the appropriate practical outworking of the gospel in the

---

[26] *Ibid.*, p. 32.   [27] *Ibid.*, p. 34.
[28] A. Harnack, *The Mission and Expansion of Christianity* (ET London and New York, vol. I, 1904, vol. II, 1905), vol. I, ch. 7.

society to which these Christians belonged and in which they had their mission.[29] Salvation in Christ meant that the law, in so far as it applied to the righteous person, was written in the heart, and the outcome of belief in the gospel was the fruit of good works. All this was the work of God's grace. Such was the simple and obvious conclusion of Paul's wrestling and argumentation for those who inherited his message in the Gentile world.

[29] Towner, *The Goal of our Instruction.*

CHAPTER 3

God and the divine activity

'The author of the Pastorals had no theology of his own. He is a purveyor of other men's theology.'[1] This comment is by no means untypical of scholarly estimate of the theology of the Pastorals. Not only is the theology generally seen to be a collection of traditions, but it is also usually treated as a fairly arbitrary, inconsistent, unthought-out amalgam with little coherence.

Some justification for this estimate may be found in the fact that many of the explicitly theological statements occur in what appear to be liturgical passages or hymns. Thus it is assumed that they express the affirmations of the community rather than a creatively formed theological position, and that they were simply lifted into the text in order to punctuate it with faith-statements. Coupled with the view that the ethics is 'autonomous', such an estimate of these passages leaves these letters a patch-work with no meaningful structure. Until recently there has been little attempt to explore the theology of the Pastorals except by comparison and contrast with the theology of Paul, but there has been a recent trend towards assessing them in their own right.[2] In the last chapter, it was

---

[1] A. T. Hanson, *Studies in the Pastoral Epistles* (London, 1968), p. 110.

[2] Lewis R. Donelson, *Pseudepigraphy and Ethical Argument in the Pastoral Epistles* (Tübingen, 1986), is the most distinguished attempt. He would also maintain that the argumentation has coherence, but the details of his analysis go beyond the immediate concern of this study, which concentrates on the theology of these letters. Other studies concentrating on the Pastorals in their own right include Norbert Brox's commentary and Towner, *The Goal of our Instruction*. Towner's focus on the soteriological and missionary concern of these epistles provides a useful approach, and his comprehensive scholarship is very valuable, despite the limitations of those parts of his study which concentrate narrowly on vocabulary studies.

47

argued that the ethics has a theological base, and that therefore there is a more consistent theology than has generally been suggested. It is time to reassess the theological material and to reconsider its function in the argument as a whole.

The project of writing a 'theology of' any particular writing is hampered by an inherent problem, namely the difficulty of avoiding an amalgam of salient features abstracted from their immediate context and organised according to categories in which the reader has an interest. No analysis can avoid this danger entirely, but we will begin by linking the epistles' theology with their primary ethical content, hoping thus to reduce such abstraction, and relevant words and phrases will always be gathered with attention to their immediate context.

IN THE SIGHT OF GOD

'This is good and acceptable in the sight of our Saviour God' (1 Tim. 2.3). This is the first of a number of times when these texts make explicit what seems to be implicit all through. The lifestyle to which the readers are called is shaped by the fact that all is from God and under God and accountable to God. If at first sight the epistles seem to be a collection of instructions without much theological material, a survey of how frequently and in what ways the word 'God' appears proves that that is a superficial reading of these letters.

It is not for nothing that the first 'doxological' passage, or liturgical aside (a stylistic feature of the authentic Paulines found also here, though the content is not in these cases characteristically Pauline), is the offering of glory and honour for ever and ever, 'To the King of the universe [or ages], the imperishable, unseen, only God' (1 Tim. 1.17). A similar doxology appears towards the end of 1 Timothy:

He is the blessed and only Sovereign, King of kings and Lord of lords; he alone possesses immortality, dwelling in unapproachable light; him no one has ever seen or can ever see; to him be honour and dominion for ever! Amen. (6.15–16)

To comment that this is clearly the language of the Hellenistic synagogue,[3] while important, is to distract from the perspective which this introduces. The King of the Universe, the One true God (1 Tim. 2.5), has all of creation in the royal purview. This God does not demand rejection of created things, but their sanctification, their proper use:

Every one of God's created things is good, and nothing is to be rejected if received with thanksgiving. For it is consecrated through the word of God and by prayer. (1 Tim. 4.4–5)

Those who believe and know the truth must recognise that God is the Creator, and what he has created is for sharing with thanksgiving (1 Tim. 4.3). That principle applies also to marriage and procreation, to the proper ordering of society, and the other concerns which are of over-riding importance to those to whom these texts belonged.

This God, the One God and King of the Universe, is concerned about all within it. Hence prayers and intercessions are to be offered for all human beings, for kings and all those in authority (1 Tim. 2.1–2). This God wants all human beings to be saved and to come to knowledge of truth (1 Tim. 2.4; cf. 4.10). This is the universal God, not a secret God known only to the spiritual elite. There is a fundamental difference between the 'knowledge falsely so-called' and the knowledge of God's way which is sketched in these texts. The opposition profess to know God, but by their actions display their misapprehensions:

To the pure all things are pure. (Titus 1.15)

Those who fail to recognise that principle are unfaithful (the Greek word *apeitheis* (Titus 1.16) may be alternatively translated as 'disobedient' or 'disbelieving', but I would suggest that the false teachers are presented as having been unfaithful to the truth they once grasped): their minds and consciences have been corrupted, so that they can no longer recognise that all

---

[3] E.g. Kelly and Dibelius–Conzelmann, where parallels are cited from Hellenistic literature, both Jewish and philosophical. For the Hellenisation of the Jews, see M. Hengel, *Judaism and Hellenism* (ET London, 1974).

things derive from the Creator. So they claim to know God, but their actions, presumably their hindering of marriage and their abstention from foods as indicated in 1 Tim. 4.3ff., belie that claim, and make them unfit for any good deed. (Titus 1.16)

This universal God is not only Creator but also Judge. Life is to be lived in the sight of God, and these texts self-consciously spell out what is acceptable in the divine sight (1 Tim. 2.3; 5.4). It is 'in the sight of God and Christ Jesus and the elect angels' that the reader is charged to keep the instructions (1 Tim. 5.21; 6.13). People are to be warned 'in God's sight' not to dispute about words (2 Tim. 2.14). The charge to preach the Word, to correct, rebuke and encourage, is given 'in the sight of God and of Christ Jesus who will judge the living and the dead' (2 Tim. 4.1). The aim is to 'present yourself to God as one approved' (a word which implies approved after proving or testing) (2 Tim. 2.15). The intercession offered in return for Onesiphorus' support is 'May the Lord grant that he will find mercy from the Lord on that day!' (2 Tim. 1.18). There is judgment to come; everything is in the Lord's sight.

But more than all else this God is a Saviour God. 'We hope in the living God, who is Saviour of all human beings, especially believers' (1 Tim. 4.10).

GOD AS SAVIOUR

It is characteristic that in the Pastorals, God is called Saviour.[4] Designation of God as Saviour happens in these texts, six out of the mere eight times the usage occurs in the entire New Testament; in addition we hear of the saving grace of God (Titus 2.11), and God is described as the one who has saved us (2 Tim. 1.9). The verb 'save' is used six times, always, except perhaps once, with God directly or indirectly the implied subject. Besides this, Christ Jesus appears as Saviour four times, and his saving activity is closely linked with the divine activity of salvation. The use of 'Saviour' to characterise God and his

---

[4] This observation is now standard among commentators, and usually provides a point of contrast with Paul. Towner's more constructive exploration of this aspect of these epistles is to be commended, especially chapter 5.

activity is one of the distinctive features of these short texts – it is not particularly Pauline. Let us begin by examining the contexts in which this feature appears.

1 Timothy 1.1, the initial greeting, describes Paul as 'Apostle of Jesus Christ according to the command of *God our Saviour*'.

1 Timothy 2.3 states that 'this', namely to spend a gentle and quiet life in all godliness and holiness, 'is good and acceptable before *our Saviour God*, who wishes all to be saved and to come to knowledge of truth'.

1 Timothy 4.10 speaks of hoping in the living God, who is *Saviour* of all human beings, especially believers.

2 Timothy 1.9 describes God as 'the one who *has saved us* and called us with a holy calling, not according to our works but according to the divine purpose and grace'. The passage goes on to speak of this plan of God being 'granted to us in Christ Jesus before ancient times and revealed now through the appearance of *our Saviour Christ Jesus*'.

2 Timothy 2.10 shows Paul enduring everything for the elect, 'in order that they might attain to the *salvation* which is in Christ Jesus with eternal glory'.

2 Timothy 4.18 expresses confidence that 'the Lord will rescue me from every wicked act [this must refer to attacks on Paul's person, given the context in the previous verses], and will bring me safe [Greek = 'save'] into his heavenly Kingdom'.

Titus 1.2–4: in the course an elaborate greeting, reference is made to the '*kerygma* with which I was entrusted according to the command of *our Saviour God*', and the greeting ends with 'grace and peace from God the Father and Christ Jesus *our Saviour*'.

Titus 2.10 suggests that slaves should behave in such a way as to show they can be trusted, so that 'they make the teaching of *our Saviour God* attractive to all'.

Titus 2.11–13 speaks of the '*saving* grace of God' appearing to all human beings. The activity of God's saving grace is said to be teaching. The teaching produces lives which refuse ungodliness and worldly desires and produce self-control, righteousness and piety. Such lives are lived in anticipation of 'the

blessed hope and the glorious appearing of the great God and
our Saviour Jesus Christ'.

Titus 3.4 sings of the appearance of 'the kindness and love
[*philanthrōpia* = love towards human beings] of *our Saviour God*'.
God is described as having '*saved* us not through works of
righteousness we had done [presumably good deeds], but,
according to the divine mercy, through the bath of re-birth
[presumably baptism] and the renewal of the Holy Spirit
which was poured out richly upon us through *Jesus Christ our
Saviour*'.

What is noticeable is that the community to which these
texts belong lays claim to the universal God in a special way as
'our Saviour God', while retaining the universal perspective.
This God wants to save all. Later we find that this God requires
behaviour that will be recognisably 'beautiful', that will
'adorn' those who profess to follow God's way (something like
this suggests the implicit meaning of Titus 2.10; 'attractive'
captures but part of the sense). Immoral, illegal, unruly or
disruptive behaviour is bound to bring the gospel into disrepute. Hence the prayers that they may live peaceful and
quiet lives in all godliness and holiness. Hence the need for a
bishop who has a good reputation outside the community, and
hence too all the regulations that are brought together in these
texts. The impression given to the outside world is important,[5]
for the way to be followed is the way of the God who is the
universal God.

However, it is especially believers who know this God as
Saviour. So believers who are true to the gospel have knowledge of the truth, and those who are being saved identify with
this community of the faithful. They have been initiated
through a cult-act, the 'bath of re-birth' (Titus 3.5), and they
submit to the disciplines and traditions of the community, a

---

[5] Towner, *The Goal of our Instruction*, notes repeatedly that the emphasis on the
impression created on outsiders has not merely a defensive note, but a missionary
intent. That may be so. Certainly these epistles would seem to present respectability
as a positive witness to the truth about the God of the universe and the lifestyle that
embodies the divine intention.

point these epistles are especially concerned to press. The one who witnesses to Christ through suffering expects rescue from his enemies in a hostile world, and to be saved *into* the heavenly kingdom (2 Tim. 4.18) – thus the content of salvation is given slightly more explicit enunciation, and its ambivalent place in the present world acknowledged.[6]

Not only do the texts progressively reinforce the particular and special relationship between this community and the universal God, but there is an interesting shift in the linguistic habit. In 1 Timothy, God is designated Saviour; the God of the universe is the one who saves. In 2 Timothy, the designation 'Saviour' is no longer attached to God; rather there are descriptions of the activity of God who saves according to a purpose or plan long mapped out, and that plan is identified with the appearance of our Saviour Jesus Christ, and consists of that salvation which is in Christ. The designation 'Saviour' has shifted to Jesus. In Titus, God is again called Saviour, but now always in close association with Jesus Christ who is also called Saviour. Indeed there is real ambiguity in Titus 2.13,[7] where it is difficult to know whether we should translate as above, retaining some distinction between God and Jesus, or whether we should translate, as most versions do, 'our God and Saviour Jesus Christ', seeing a transfer of both 'Saviour' and 'God' to Jesus.

There seems to be, then, a crescendo of focus on the saving work of Christ as constituting the saving activity of God the Saviour, but that should not mislead us into supposing that this is not there from the start. The gospel of salvation through Christ is already sketched early in 1 Timothy: **1 Timothy 1.12–17** depicts Paul as the one whom 'Christ Jesus our Lord empowered' for his service, despite his earlier persecution of the church. 'The grace of our Lord overflowed with the faith and love which is in Christ Jesus. The saying is trustworthy and

---

[6] See further discussion on pp. 56ff.

[7] A comprehensive review of the arguments, and the various scholars supporting each side of the case, is to be found now in the commentary of George W. Knight III in the New International Greek Testament Commentary (Grand Rapids and Carlisle, 1992), pp. 322ff. Dibelius–Conzelmann and Kelly support the view taken here.

worthy of complete acceptance, that Christ Jesus came into the world to save sinners, of which I am the first.' Thus Paul becomes the paradigm of a saved sinner, and the source of salvation is vested in the coming of Christ.

It is also clear that the greetings of the three epistles encapsulate the sense of God and Christ being involved together in the salvation process, but put side by side they too manifest a kind of crescendo (it is worth while comparing carefully 1 Tim. 1.1–2; 2 Tim. 1.1–2 and Titus 1.1–4). The elaborated greeting in Titus picks up 'our Saviour God' from 1 Timothy, but spells out much more fully the effects of salvation in the community, linking in Christ Jesus, also 'our Saviour'. The letters seem to display a concern both to hold to a universal vision and to affirm a special relationship and a special responsibility within that, first for Paul, then for those for whom Paul is a paradigm. Through Jesus Christ, the universal God is '*our* Saviour God'.

Furthermore, this Saviour God has a plan in which both Paul and the community have a role to play. The passages already surveyed make this clear (particularly 2 Tim. 1.9), and perhaps should encourage us to interpret 1 Timothy 1.4 as referring to this plan in the phrase *oikonomia theou*.

Commentaries suggest two different ways of taking this: (1) There is a variant reading, *oikodomē*, which has a meaning to do with 'building up', or 'edifying'. A few later parallels appear to have justified taking *oikonomia* as 'training', which would appear to fit well in the context, and would explain the variant reading which clarifies the sense.[8] (2) A more normal use of the word would suggest that it means 'plan', and in Ephesians we seem to find it meaning 'God's plan of salvation'.[9]

Accepting this second sense in general terms,[10] I wonder whether another element should perhaps be considered: *oikonomia* has the root meaning 'household management', and in 1

---

[8] So RSV/NRSV. This view is favoured by Hanson, and considered by Dibelius–Conzelmann and Houlden, who reach no certain conclusion.

[9] REB. Kelly and Barrett prefer this view.

[10] See also the discussion in the commentary of George W. Knight III. Building on articles concerning usage in Colossians and Ephesians by Reumann and Moule, he suggests that it refers here to 'the outworking, administration, or stewardship of God's plan of salvation through the gospel and its communication' (p. 76).

Cor. 9.1, it seems to mean 'stewardship', as it does in a Lucan parable (Luke 16.2–4). It certainly acquired the meaning 'plan of salvation' in Christian usage, and later could even be taken to refer specifically to the incarnation.[11] In the context of these letters, the *episkopos* is the *oikonomos theou* in the *oikos theou*; so one wonders whether the 'household' metaphor does not link all these usages. Is the *episkopos* the servant-administrator or steward of God's household, charged with executing God's *oikonomia* or plan? In which case, 1 Tim. 1.4 presumably refers to all the lifestyle, order, indeed 'training' and discipline of service spelt out in these letters as appropriate for members of God's household. It is this which is threatened by the speculations of the false teachers. In other words, as Donelson suggests, the debate about the meaning of *oikonomia* is rather unnecessary.[12] To accept this exegesis is to acknowledge that God's 'economy' or plan of salvation is paramount for these epistles, and the ordering of God's household is clearly part of the outworking of that plan.

All this material demonstrates that salvation is all-important for these epistles, as both Towner and Donelson have argued.[13] Donelson suggests, however, that Christology is subsumed in this plan of God, Jesus Christ being confined to his two 'epiphanies' so as to reduce over-enthusiasm about the living Christ.[14] We have ourselves noted some ambiguities about the naming of God and Christ. Soon we must turn to Christology, but first we need to consider what exactly these epistles mean by salvation.

---

[11] A brief summary of later theological usage is found under 'economy' in *A New Dictionary of Christian Theology*, ed. Alan Richardson and John Bowden (London, 1983). Eastern theology from the fourth century distinguished between *theologia*, referring to God in the essential divine Being (as Trinity), and *oikonomia*, referring to God's providential (administrative!) outreach to the world in creation, revelation and incarnation (in which the whole Trinity was involved, with one will and purpose).

[12] Donelson, *Pseudepigraphy and Ethical Argument*, p. 133.

[13] Towner, *The Goal of our Instruction*, especially chapter 5; for Donelson, *Pseudepigraphy and Ethical Argument*, the salvation-theme provides 'cosmological' warrant for the ethical instruction.

[14] Donelson, *Pseudepigraphy and Ethical Argument*, pp. 133–54.

SALVATION

These little epistles, it has often been noted by commentators, are punctuated by 'faithful sayings'. Sometimes it is difficult to determine whether the standard phrase 'faithful is the saying' refers to what has gone immediately before or what follows immediately after, but what is evident, I submit, is that the formula is invariably attached to a statement about salvation.[15] This would suggest that the phrase does not simply signal a reliable Pauline tradition, or a secure doctrine, but rather heralds an assurance of the gospel.[16] Perhaps we should translate *logos* not simply as 'saying' but as 'word', meaning the Word of the Lord.

1 Timothy 1.15, the first example of a 'faithful saying', is a much-quoted text, precisely because it is a summary of the gospel, and it is introduced by the most elaborate signal: not only is the word sure, but it is worthy of full acceptance, and it tells that 'Christ Jesus came into the world to save sinners.'

1 Timothy 3.1 is a case where the reference is disputed. Some think 'the word is sure' is a remark concluding the previous section, others refer it to the following statement about the bishop. If my suggestion about the link between these sayings and salvation proves convincing, that would settle the point:

---

[15] This suggestion is canvassed by Dibelius–Conzelmann and, according to Hanson's commentary (p. 63, cf. p. 36), argued by W. Nauck in a Göttingen dissertation of 1950.

[16] All commentators treat the 'faithful sayings' as in some sense quotations. Kelly (p. 54) refers to the solemn ring of the formula which introduces a 'citation, probably drawn from early catechetical or liturgical material'. J. L. Houlden, *The Pastoral Epistles* (London and Philadelphia, 1989) (p. 60) regards this favourite phrase as a way of drawing attention to 'key doctrinal statements'. George W. Knight III (p. 99) notes that 'in each occurrence the statement to which the formula refers has a "saying" quality', and since *logos* can mean a 'saying', he deduces that the phrase is a quotation formula, referring to his own study, *The Faithful Sayings in the Pastoral Letters* (Kampen, 1968; Grand Rapids, 1979). On *pistos* he suggests that 'Paul ... is saying that it is a faithful presentation of God's message', and cross-references 2 Tim. 2.2, as well as 2 Cor. 1.15–23. This comment moves towards my suggestion that *logos* may well refer to God's Word or the gospel, rather than simply mean 'saying'. Hanson (p. 63) is unconvinced by most suggestions as to coherent theme or purpose, concluding that 'he employs it to link traditional material with his present situation'.

the previous statement is about woman being saved by child-bearing, provided she has the right character.

1 Timothy 4.9 is another case where the reference is unclear, but either way it evidences the link. If it refers back, it is about *eusebeia* which holds promise for the present life and the life to come, which, as we shall see is what salvation is all about; if it refers forward, it is about hope in the living God who is the Saviour of all.

2 Timothy 2.11 is embedded in a salvation context; it follows reference to obtaining the salvation which is in Christ Jesus, with eternal glory, and probably introduces the following hymnic or credal passage about dying and rising, enduring and reigning with Christ.

Titus 3.8: here the phrase must refer back, and once again it is a lengthy celebration of the saving activity of God evidenced in baptism and the outpouring of the Holy Spirit through Jesus Christ which is being celebrated and guaranteed.

The so-called 'faithful sayings' are words of salvation. Of salvation there is no definition as such in the Pastoral epistles, but we can glean what it is supposed to consist in by careful attention to these and other passages we have already referred to. The nearest to a definitive statement would appear to be in Titus 2.11–14, which speaks of the saving grace of God appearing, and

by it we are trained to refuse ungodliness and worldly desires, and to live a life of self-control, righteousness and piety in the present age, looking forward to the blessed hope and the glorious appearing of the great God and our Saviour Jesus Christ. He it is who gave himself for us, to set us free from all wickedness and to purify for himself a chosen people, eager to do good.

In summary we might say that salvation is the gift and attainment of that perfection which will inherit eternal life. God's plan is to enable that outcome for all humankind.

There are two obvious aspects, future and present, and each has its obverse. In the end, acquittal at the Final Judgment constitutes salvation, the obverse being condemnation. The

outcome of acquittal will be to receive the crown of righteousness, and the inheritance of eternal life, immortality,
eternal glory. This eschatological dimension of salvation,
however, has its present aspect. That future depends on life
now lived in God's sight and judged according to God's will.
Hence the importance of the proper ordering of life in community, which, if not explicitly, at least by implication mirrors or
anticipates God's heavenly kingdom. The disciple of Christ is
to learn how to live according to God's 'economy',[17] in contentment, accepting his or her place and role in the proper
order of things. Thus the social well-being produced by living
according to the will of the Creator is an aspect of salvation, as
is the development of the character and behaviour that fosters
peace and harmony, with respect and obedience paid to God
through respecting and obeying those who are the divine
representatives, together with faithfulness under pressure and
loyalty when tested. The obverse of this is insubordination,
disruptive and disloyal behaviour, which is roundly condemned (1 Tim. 6.3–5; 2 Tim. 3.2ff.; Titus 1.10–16; 3.9–11).

This salvation is both gift and attainment. It is gift in the
sense that it is the result of God's grace in Christ, and it came
with his 'epiphany', a fact which carries with it the assumption
that it brought peace and joy, plenty and fulfilment (see
further the next section). It is received through the bath of
rebirth, through redemption and purification, and through
renewal by the Holy Spirit (Titus 3.4–7). This grace has been
revealed through our Saviour Christ Jesus, who has destroyed
death and has brought life and immortality to light through
the Gospel (1 Tim. 1.10). It is being called with a holy calling
(2 Tim. 1.9ff.) and brought safe into God's heavenly kingdom
(2 Tim. 4.18). But salvation is also attainment because to reach
it demands the response of loyalty, faithfulness under pressure,
the testimony of the believer, and the obedient life lived
according to God's will. Salvation involves knowledge of the
truth that leads to godliness (Titus 1.1), and the church is a
learning community in which Christian character is formed.

---

[17] See above, pp. 54–5.

Paul's metaphor of household vessels, some for wrath, some for mercy (Rom. 9.22) appears in a new guise: in a house are to be found vessels of gold and silver, wood and clay, for good or ignoble purposes – every vessel is to cleanse its own self so as to be an instrument for noble purposes, made holy, useful to the Master, ready for any good work (2 Tim. 2.20–1).

This training in righteousness is what these epistles hope to foster, but as we saw in the previous chapter, salvation depends upon God's mercy, and that gift is mediated by Christ. So what do these epistles have to say about the status and role of Jesus Christ?

CHRISTOLOGY

Let us begin with the ambiguities. As we have seen, the title 'Saviour' is first attributed to God, and then shifts to Christ, and is then applied to both together. It is instructive to look also at *kyrios*, 'Lord'.

In Titus, the title *kyrios* never appears: the designation 'Saviour' dominates the text, now applied to Christ as well as God, as we have seen.

In 1 Tim. 1.2, 12; 6.3 and 6.14, however, 'Lord' is indisputably used of Jesus Christ. In this letter where, as we have seen, 'Saviour' belongs to God, God's title, *kyrios*, is usually applied to Christ. Once, but only once, is the attribution unclear, namely in 1.14, where the context strongly suggests that Christ is as usual intended, the whole paragraph being about 'Christ Jesus our Lord' and his saving activity. So 'the grace of our Lord' which 'has overflowed with faith and the love which is in Christ Jesus', would seem to be the grace of Christ, but could be God's grace.[18]

In 2 Timothy the same attribution of 'Lord' to Christ appears at the start, both in the greeting, 1.2, and presumably in 1.8: this refers in the same instant to the 'witness of our Lord' and Paul's imprisonment, suggesting the phrase is parallel in

---

[18] Most commentators see no distinction, referring to the divine grace known in Christ. George W. Knight III sets out arguments on either side, and agrees with the view taken here.

sense to 1 Tim. 6.13 (describing Christ's martyr-witness before Pilate). But thereafter there is undoubted ambiguity. In 1.18, we read:

May the Lord grant that he find mercy from the Lord on that day.

Do both uses of the word *kyrios* refer to the same Lord? And which is referred to? In 2.7, a Proverb is quoted:

For the Lord will give you understanding in everything.

In its original context, Proverbs 2.6, this must have referred to God; but what about here? In 2 Tim. 2.22 there is a reference to those 'who call on the Lord from a clean heart', which sounds as though it should refer to God, but two verses later we learn that the 'slave of the Lord' should not fight; which reference now? In chapter 4, we find the title associated with the Final Judgment, as 1.18 presumably did:

For the rest, the crown of righteousness awaits me, with which the Lord will reward me on that day, the righteous judge, and not only me but also all those who love his 'epiphany'. (4.8)

We might guess that this is a reference to Christ's Parousia, when he was expected to act on God's behalf as Judge, and that may affect our decision about the reference of the earlier cases. If so, that view might be confirmed by the next occurrence, in 4.17, where the Lord is described as 'empowering me', a function attributed to Christ Jesus in 1 Timothy 1.12. But the ambiguity remains in 4.18:

The Lord will rescue me from every bad deed and will bring me safe into his heavenly kingdom; to whom be glory for ever and ever, Amen.

It sounds like a reminiscence of 2 Cor. 1.10, but the previous verse in the 2 Corinthians context demonstrates that the one who is to save Paul from death is 'the God who raises the dead'. Furthermore, the doxology here in 2 Timothy suggests that God may be in mind. The final words of this letter are, 'The Lord be with your spirit. Grace be with you.' Again the reference is unclear.

So far then we have noted further differences between these

three little letters in their linguistic habits of referring to God and Christ, and found further confirmation that there is a certain ambiguity because their activity is seen as one. We must turn to a review of the clearly Christological passages to try and discern how their relationship is understood, and so how this ambiguity might be resolved.

The key passages are often doxological or hymn-like interjections, difficult to translate, allusive in quality, so that of many of them it is hard to provide a clear and definite exegesis. Let us begin by assembling in full passages of this character, setting them out in a way that highlights this credal or poetic quality. It is important for assessing the theology of these letters to 'experience' the material in this way. For we need to determine the extent to which it has the ring of liturgical tradition, and therefore defies analysis in terms of a systematic doctrine.

1 Timothy 2.5–6

> For God is One,
> One also is the mediator between God and human beings,
> the human person, Christ Jesus,
> who gave himself as a ransom for many,
> the testimony at the proper time.

1 Timothy 3.16

> Who appeared in flesh,
> was justified in spirit,
> revealed to angels,
> was preached among Gentiles,
> believed in the world,
> was assumed in glory.

1 Timothy 6.13ff.

I charge you, in the sight of God who generates life in all things, and of Christ Jesus who bore testimony to the noble confession under Pontius Pilate, that you keep the commandment unspotted and blameless until the 'epiphany' of our Lord Jesus Christ, which in his own good time, God will display,

> the blessed and only Master,
> King of kings,

> the One who alone has immortality,
> dwelling in unapproachable light,
> whom no human being has seen or can see;
> to whom be glory and eternal might, Amen.

2 Timothy 1.9–10

> [God] the one who has saved us
> and called us with a holy calling,
> not according to our works
> but according to his own plan and grace,
> which was given to us in Christ Jesus
> before eternal times,
> and appeared now
> through the 'epiphany' of our Saviour Christ Jesus
> who brought death to nothing
> and brought life and immortality to light through the Gospel ...

2 Timothy 2.11–13

> Faithful is the saying:
> For if we die with him we shall live with him;
> If we endure, we will also reign;
> If we deny, he will also deny us;
> If we are unfaithful, he will remain faithful,
> For he cannot deny himself.

Titus 3.4–7

> When it was made apparent – the kindness and love
> of our Saviour God,
> not because of works of righteousness
> which we had performed,
> but because of his mercy,
> he saved us by the bath of re-birth
> and renewal of the Holy Spirit,
> which he poured out richly upon us
> through Jesus Christ our Saviour,
> that justified by his grace
> we might become heirs according to the hope of eternal life.

Looking at the first of these passages, one might be tempted
to think that the theology of these epistles is founded on a
highly transcendent, even remote, understanding of the One
universal God, and that the function of Christ is to be mediator

in the sense of bridging the gap. This might be felt to be confirmed by the final passage from the same letter (1 Tim. 6.13ff.); God is beyond the sight of human eye, hidden in unapproachable light, and communication comes through a kind of delegate. This is so unlike Paul's theology that it sharply highlights the unlikelihood that he had much hand in the composition of these letters.

While it is impossible to deny something of this picture, two things alert us to the fact that it has to be nuanced a bit. The first is that the dynamic engagement of God in the salvation process is implied throughout. The divine initiative is transparent, not only in establishing a pre-prepared plan, but in the attribution of the term 'Saviour' to God, and in the sense that everything is played out in God's sight, and accomplished through God's providence. The second is precisely the ambiguities already noted. As mediator, Christ is the immanence or appearance of the invisible God, which means that in a real sense Christ stands for God, taking over God's functions, with the focus on judging, it would seem, in 2 Timothy, and on saving in Titus. Titles are interchangeable, and often there is no clear differentiation: the Lord (Christ) is for human beings the Lord (God). This 'agency' Christology is not all that far from Paul's theology, and so may be regarded as a legitimate development of it in an environment shaped by Hellenistic Judaism. It might appear to subordinate Jesus Christ,[19] but could also be read in a more representative way, whereby Christ is the communication of the transcendent God within the created order.[20]

Christ as God's agent has two 'epiphanies', it seems. The first is as a human being, in flesh; the second is as Judge at the End. The 'epiphany' Christology of these letters is one aspect that

---

[19] Donelson argues this, *Pseudepigraphy and Ethical Argument*, p. 135.

[20] Towner, *The Goal of our Instruction*, pp. 53–4, has an interesting discussion, suggesting that *mesitēs* had attracted covenant-ideas to itself (cf. Heb. 8.6; 9.15; 12.24). This would reinforce and particularise the point made in this paragraph, though the Pastorals do not refer anywhere to 'covenant'. A link in ideas may be expressed in Titus 2.14, 'purifying a people', since the new covenant passage in Jer. 31.31ff., referred to in both Paul and Hebrews, suggests purification of former sins prior to the 'mediation' of the covenant in the spirit.

links significantly with the emphasis on salvation we have already explored;[21] for the association between salvation and epiphany has been found in the Hellenistic background.

The classic discussion is to be found in Adolf Deissmann, *Light from the Ancient East*,[22] where material was collected, some of it then of recent discovery, which showed how many extraordinary parallels exist between the vocabulary of the 'ruler-cult' and early Christology. In an official inscription, the town council of Ephesus spoke of Julius Caesar as 'the God made manifest, offspring of Ares and Aphrodite, and common saviour of human life' (pp. 348–9); fragments of a marble pedestal from Pergamum bear an inscription concerning Augustus, 'The Emperor, Caesar, son of a god, the god Augustus, of every land and sea the overseer (*epoptēn*)' (p. 350). In the Eastern Empire, the emperors were called *kyrios*, 'Lord', from early in the first century, as is evidenced from many inscriptions, ostraca and papyri (p. 357), 'King of kings and Lord of lords' is also paralleled, and the title 'Saviour' or 'Saviour of the world' was bestowed on Julius Caesar, Augustus, Claudius, Vespasian, Titus, Trajan, Hadrian and other emperors in Eastern inscriptions (p. 369).

But it is not just a matter of titles: *Euangelion* is used in a particularly significant inscription in Priene concerning the birthday of the god Augustus (pp. 370–1). *Parousia* was associated with the 'advent' of a king or emperor from the time of the Ptolemaic kings of Egypt, and continued into the time of the Roman Empire. The imperial 'visit' began a new era, which might be described as salvation for his people, special coins were struck, and inscriptions were set up. Such a visit could also be called the manifestation or 'epiphany' of the king (pp. 372–8). To be the 'slave of Christ', given all these associations, must have provoked comparison with being one of the many imperial slaves; to be ambassador of Christ was like being ambassador of the emperor.

---

[21] See above, pp. 50–9.
[22] Originally published in Tübingen, 1908, as *Licht vom Osten*, the 2nd edition being translated into English by L. R. M. Strachan, and published in 1910.

More than other New Testament texts[23] the Pastorals evidence the language that so intriguingly parallels the 'ruler-cult'. As the emperor was god by being son of a god or the manifestation of a god, so Christ is Lord and God as God's Son, or God's manifestation. When Christ visits the earth, God appears. The gospel, the good news is about that divine epiphany. The divine epiphany brings safety or salvation to the people.

Given the parallels, it is not unreasonable to suggest that there is a deliberate placing of this Christ-cult against the Caesar-cult,[24] as the universal gospel to which beleaguered aliens bear witness, and suffer for it (the notion of Christians having citizenship elsewhere does not appear in the Pastorals, but is found in other early Christian texts (e.g. Phil. 3.20; 1 Clem. 2) and is perhaps implied by the 'kingdom language' and, e.g., 2 Tim. 2.3–4). It explains the theological phenomena we have noted: this Saviour Christ is the true, universal Saviour, manifested according to the providential plan of the universal God who is Saviour of all, but this Lord demands exclusive loyalty, and is therefore not only the universal Saviour but the particular Saviour and Lord of those who entrust themselves to his plan. His 'epiphany' as the man Jesus Christ, and his return as Lord and Judge, rival the claims of Lord Caesar, Saviour of the world; and Christ's slaves and servants should not be ashamed of the chains they may have to wear as subversives in the Caesar's empire.

The effect of this Christology, therefore, is both to articulate the public character of the Christian claim, thus differentiating it from the esoteric claims of the false teachers, and also to validate the sense of being in the world but not of the world, of

---

[23] The nearest is perhaps 2 Peter, also regarded as a late document within the New Testament.

[24] The context of the Hellenistic ruler-cult is acknowledged in Dibelius–Conzelmann, Kelly, etc. Not all commentators, however, give weight to these parallels, especially those who focus on the Old Testament background to the theological terminology of these letters, e.g. George W. Knight. Syncretistic influence is probably not convincing, given that the theological background is clearly Hellenistic Judaism, probably mediated through the Christian community. An underlying parody deliberately adopted in the service of the gospel is another matter, however. See Towner's discussion, *The Goal of our Instruction*, p. 77.

needing to bear a testimony that may lead to confrontation. Christ himself bore such a testimony (1 Tim. 6.13ff.).

Some of the hymn-like passages I have quoted above include this dimension – note 2 Tim. 2.11–13 in particular, which speaks of dying with him, so as to live with him, enduring with him so as to reign with him. But the notion of Christ's testimony, or martyr-witness, before Pontius Pilate seems to be less obviously traditional, and not only not anticipated in Paul, but also more embedded in the material attributable to those who compiled these documents. In the hymn-like passages, Christ's work of salvation is described in traditional (though not necessarily distinctively Pauline) terms, such as: giving himself as a ransom for many, bringing death to nought and bringing life and immortality to light, saving through the bath of rebirth and the renewal of the Holy Spirit poured out on us, justifying by grace and making heirs, etc. Such pictures are summed up in the faithful saying that Christ came into the world to save sinners (1 Tim. 1.15), a point demonstrated by the paradigm of Paul himself. But the distinctive notion of Christ's testimony, of Jesus making the noble confession as a paradigm of the call of the 'man of God', provides the climax of 1 Timothy (6.13, and note how it is integrated into the sequence from verse 11). It is from that climax that 2 Timothy takes off.

For 2 Timothy opens by tackling the issue of being ashamed, whether of our Lord's testimony[25] or of 'me, his prisoner'. After all, it is a disgrace to be on the wrong side of the law. One might well be ashamed to be associated with those who are, especially as there has been in 1 Timothy a celebration of law and order as an aspect of God's good creation. The need to face with courage the possibility of suffering (2 Tim. 1.7–8) is picked up in the military metaphor:

Take your share of hardship as a fine soldier of Christ Jesus. No-one on active service can be distracted by the everyday affairs of life, if he is to please his commander. (2 Tim. 2.3–4)

---

[25] Or perhaps 'your testimony to our Lord' (REB), but this surely detracts from the point, and certainly obviates the possibility of a link between the argument here and Christ's testimony before Pilate in 1 Tim. 6.13.

And 'Paul', it is pressed a few verses later, was exposed to hardship, even to the point of being fettered like a criminal (2.9). Such is the noble confession of which even Christ, the commander, is an example. Confrontation with the powers that be is likely for those who take Christ as leader and Saviour rather than the emperor.

So we seem to have a picture of Christ as the Lord and King who is the manifestation of the transcendent invisible King of the Universe, the only eternal God. Like the emperor, he pays 'visits' to his subjects. Does this imply, as Donelson argues,[26] a presently absent Christ?

First of all, he banishes Jesus from the scene ... In place of the uncontrollable presence and authority of Jesus speaking in visions [the position Donelson attributes to the false teachers], the author inserts an epiphany Christology where Jesus is relegated to two appearances, one in the past and one in the future, with no present contact. Contact with Jesus comes through adherence to correct doctrine, which in turn comes through obedience to the leaders of the author's faction in the church. In Jesus' place stand his designated representatives. Secondly, quiet virtues constitute the sole means of salvation. Knowledge, spiritualism, ascetic practices, and even baptism are of no avail if the quiet virtues are not practiced ... God's plan of salvation, the entire purpose of creation, and the impact of Jesus himself, all focus upon living a quiet and peaceful life which successfully practices the more communal Greco-Roman virtues, producing health and peace in the church.

Donelson is suggesting, then, that Christ is absent until his next visit, and meanwhile authority is vested in his delegates, Paul, Timothy, Titus and their successors, each commissioned in succession from Christ to pass on the right teaching as the community awaits the return of its King. Such a picture, he implies, would be explained by the stand-point of the false teachers.

Two considerations would modify a picture painted in such an extreme fashion, though in general terms it does illuminate the assumptions that seem to lie behind these letters. The first is a point drawn out earlier, namely, the evident sense of being

---

[26] Donelson, *Pseudepigraphy and Ethical Argument*, p. 153.

engaged in a tussle in which Christ has led the way, and remains commander. The analogy of a military operation explains delegation to subordinate officers, one might say, but there is a very lively sense of being under the eye of the Lord and accountable to him in the end. He is not so absent that the troops can disregard him. The second is the presence of the Holy Spirit. Clearly we need to pursue further the understanding of the Spirit found in these letters, and their eschatology.

THE HOLY SPIRIT

The word *pneuma* appears but seven times in these letters, and evidences the range of meanings found in Paul and elsewhere in the New Testament. Just as in English we can use the word 'spirit' in a variety of ways and contexts in everyday language (e.g. 'high spirits', 'the spirit of the team', etc.), so too in Greek, and it is important not to jump to the conclusion that the word is always used in a highly theological sense. When we read in 2 Tim. 1.7, 'God has not given us a spirit of cowardice', or perhaps 'a cowardly spirit', we may presume we are dealing with such a neutral, unspecialised expression. When in 2 Tim. 4.2 we read 'the Lord be with your spirit', we are presumably dealing with a way of saying 'you', or 'your inner being'.

It is, of course, a different matter when 1 Timothy speaks of the 'spirit' warning against misleading spirits and demon-inspired doctrines (4.1). Here we have entered a world of spiritual powers in competition, the prophetic spirit predicting false prophets inspired by false spirits. A different approach again may be required to interpret the dense little 'hymn' in 1 Tim. 3.16: 'He was manifested in flesh, vindicated in spirit.' Are we speaking of two different 'realms' of 'flesh' and of 'spirit'? Or of a personal dualism? The first phrase would appear to express the incarnation, the second, the resurrection or ascension, but the phrases are so condensed as to make interpretation conjectural.

By now we have covered most of the references, and only one could conceivably refer to the divine Spirit, namely the one implying prophecy. Rather like this is the description of scripture as 'God-breathed', *theopneustos*, in 2 Timothy, a notion hardly surprising given the background in Hellenistic Judaism, where the inspiration of scripture was normally attributed to the Spirit of God.[27] The remaining two uses of *pneuma* certainly refer to the Spirit of God: in 2 Tim. 1.14 the reader is invited to 'guard the noble tradition through the holy spirit dwelling in you'; in Titus 3.5 we are told 'he saved us ... through the renewing of the holy spirit'.

These texts are the only hints as to exactly how these letters envisage the Holy Spirit at work in the church, and both indicate that what the Holy Spirit is, is the divine power to effect those things which lead to salvation. It could almost be the opposite of the 'cowardly spirit', a kind of internal driving force, but given the general usage in early Christianity that seems a little implausible. It is the Spirit of holiness sent by God to generate holiness in God's household. That holiness is shown in the lifestyle mapped out in these epistles, and in guarding the teaching tradition which facilitates that lifestyle.

Is the Spirit then channelled through the bearers of the tradition? In 2 Tim. 1.6, Timothy appears to have received God's *charisma* from Paul through the laying-on of hands.[28] In 1 Tim. 5.22, we find instructions not to lay on hands in haste, and 1 Tim. 4.14 speaks of 'the *charisma* in you which was given through prophecy by the laying on of hands of the presbyterate'. So what is this *charisma*? Is it the gift of reading, exhortation and instruction? That is what in context 1 Tim. 4.14 might suggest. But the context of the first, 2 Tim. 1.6, might suggest the opposite of the 'cowardly spirit' mentioned in the succeeding verse, and 1 Timothy 5.22 is in a context of concern lest the holiness of the authorised leader be compromised by a wrong choice of successor. So it is conceivable that the power of the Holy Spirit, which enables the maintenance of the tradition, is regarded as transmitted in this ritual act.

[27] Cf. 2 Peter 1.21. Dibelius–Conzelmann and Kelly note the idea in Josephus, *C. Apionem* 1.37ff., and Philo *Spec. Leg.* 1.65, 4.49; *Quis rer. div.* 263ff.
[28] *Charisma* simply means 'gift' – Paul uses it for the gifts of the Spirit in 1 Cor. 12. The question is whether the word has come to mean some kind of transmittable power or

The problem with that, however, is that, while one reference to the Holy Spirit speaks of guarding the noble tradition, the other refers to renewal in baptism, and that must apply to all baptised believers who are faithful to the teaching. Here too the language is of rebirth, of becoming heirs to eternal life, of the gratuitous kindness of God, of power 'poured out upon us through Jesus Christ our Saviour'. A simple identification between such gifts and good order or sound teaching is hardly plausible, even if these gifts may be jeopardised by failure to adhere to the lifestyle propounded. It is too easy to flatten the meaning of these epistles. The Holy Spirit's activity may not be discerned in ecstatic and disorderly spiritual phenomena (which may have been seen as signs of the Spirit by the false teachers[29]), but the tradition that the Spirit empowers the life of the Christian is far from dead. The Spirit of Christ is present and active, bearing fruit in the life of the church, which lives between the 'epiphanies'.

ESCHATOLOGY

This chapter began by surveying the passages which suggest that all life is lived in God's world, and in God's sight. This made it clear enough that the epistle looks forward to a final judgment. Acquittal was also found to be an important aspect of salvation. The present age is understood to be the Last Days, the present times to be unique since now is the final epoch of history.[30]

Indeed, it is evident that there is a focus upon the second 'epiphany' of 'our Lord Jesus Christ', and some of the salvation language is in the future tense: there is the suggestion that the woman *will* be saved by child-bearing (1 Tim. 2.15), that by doing what the letters urge, 'you *will* save yourself and your hearers' (1 Tim. 4.16), and the expectation that 'the Lord *will* save me into his heavenly kingdom' (2 Tim. 4.18). There is also the wish that Onesiphorus find mercy on that day (2 Tim.

---

authority to do the job for which one is commissioned by the laying-on of hands. Hanson connects this with 'institutionalisation'.

[29] Donelson, *Pseudepigraphy and Ethical Argument*, p. 153; see above, p. 67.
[30] See Towner, *The Goal of our Instruction*, p. 64ff.

1.18), and the confidence that the Lord *will* give rest (2 Tim. 2.7). The scriptures have power to lead to salvation through Jesus Christ (2 Tim. 3.15), which implies it still lies ahead. In fact, the Final Judgment is 'a major warrant' for the ethical teaching of these epistles, as Donelson notes,[31] for perseverance and faithfulness in the way set out in these letters will result in salvation which is still to be realised in the future. The notion that the Pastorals have lost urgency because of a delay in the Parousia and a tendency to settle down in the world runs counter to the evidence in the texts.[32]

It is characteristic of these letters to use *epiphaneia* instead of *parousia*, but otherwise the eschatology is very like that found in the later New Testament documents, and other early Christian texts. The present life of the community is 'between the times', we might say. The eschatological tension of Paul and the gospels has been simplified, but it is still there.[33] True, the past coming of Christ 'saved us through the bath of re-birth' (Titus 3.5); true, Paul, the chief of sinners, provided the first occasion for Christ Jesus, who came into the world to save sinners, to display his inexhaustible patience (1 Tim. 1.15–16), and others are to be saved as he was. But it is always possible to forfeit these benefits, as Hymenaeus and Alexander did, making shipwreck of their faith (1 Tim. 1.19–20).

So God repays for deeds, and the opposition will eventually be discovered, like Jannes and Jambres (2 Tim. 3.8). The truth will out, and God will deal with Alexander the coppersmith as he deserves (2 Tim. 4.14). The Lord will also crown those who deserve it. Besides all the passages noted which suggest that everything is under God's sight, two texts may sum up for us the perspective of these epistles:

1 Timothy 5.24–5

The sins of some persons are obvious, preceding them to judgement, though some their offences pursue; likewise good deeds too are obvious, but those that are not cannot be hidden.

---

[31] Donelson, *Pseudepigraphy and Ethical Argument*, p. 148.
[32] The point is well argued by Kidd, *Wealth and Beneficence*, especially chapter 4; and Towner, *The Goal of our Instruction*, especially chapter 4.
[33] Barrett, *The Pastoral Epistles*, pp. 23–4.

2 Timothy 4.7–8

I have fought the good fight, I have completed the course, I have kept
the faith; for the rest the crown of righteousness lies before me, with
which the Lord, the righteous Judge, will reward me on that day, and
not only me but also all those who love his 'epiphany'.

This focus on judgment and reward is particularly characteristic of 2 Timothy, where faithfulness, especially when loyalty is
tested by hardship and suffering, is particularly in view. This
observation raises the question whether there is a noticeable
progression in the theology of these epistles towards its own
climax. This would seem to be a question that might tie
together the themes of this chapter.

CONCLUSION

We have noted a number of interesting differences between
these three little documents. Have they been composed to more
of a plan than at first meets the eye?

In a strange kind of way, it does seem as if 1 and 2 Timothy
have different themes, and Titus, while repeating and reinforc-
ing material that has gone before, devotes proportionately
more effort to affirming the theological undergirding. The
opening of 1 Timothy is a greeting in which God is described as
Saviour and Christ as 'our hope'. It develops a perspective in
which Christ 'visits' the world on behalf of the transcendent,
invisible but Creator God to bring salvation and teach people
how to order their lives in God's household, this world being a
good place created by God. However, 2 Timothy acknowl-
edges the hostility of a world which does not receive the
message, warns of judgment, both for the opposing world and
the unfaithful, and looks forward to eternal life, to the crown-
ing reward which judgment will bring for those who have stuck
the course and not been ashamed to make their confession,
even if it means suffering and shame.

Titus, still with false teaching and unfaithfulness in focus,
repeats instructions in summary fashion, but has enlarged its
opening greeting to function as a more rounded confession of

major points of faith, and provides overall a climax or peroration affirming the basic argument. It is summed up in 2.11–15, as we have seen. The summary provokes recall of the points that have gone before: (1) the Saviour God, with the divine grace, kindness and forbearance, (2) the Saviour Christ, God's representative, who died to save the human race making his own confession before the hostile world, (3) salvation for the life of goodness in this present age, (4) membership of God's people, (5) hope for the second 'epiphany' and (6) the chain of authority ensuring that people keep faith.

And a few verses later, one of the liturgical passages from which phrases have been repeatedly drawn in this chapter reiterates this perspective, deliberately contrasting it with a past of folly, disobedience, slavery to passion, malice and envy. Often taken as the quotation of a credal confession or hymn, Titus 3.4–7 apparently echoes a kind of Pauline theology in slogans married with non-Pauline traditional language, while at the same time presenting the deeper theological perspective of these epistles. 'Such are the points I want you to insist on', we read in the following verse (Titus 3.8). So here in Titus 3.4–7 is the climax, and it is a theological confession. These epistles may not make sense as Pauline theology, but they do have a theology of their own.

CHAPTER 4

The importance of sound teaching or What about doctrinal orthodoxy?

The fundamental interest of the Pastorals would appear to be 'healthy' or 'sound teaching'. Eight times in all, we find concern for the 'health' of teaching or words, or anxiety that church members be 'healthy' in faith. Since the frequent references to 'teaching' are often translated as 'doctrine', the impression is created that orthodoxy is a primary issue, and this contributes to the usual overall estimate of scholars that the Pastorals date from a period when early charismatic freedom was being curbed by institutionalisation and by what is often referred to as 'early catholicism'.[1] Unlike the authentic Paulines, it is said, real argument with the opposition is absent, and the authoritative tradition is simply affirmed against the false-teachers. This is one reason why it is so difficult to determine exactly what the opposition believed; it also feeds the view that the Pastorals, though implicitly dogmatic, are not very theological, a view we have already contested in the previous chapter.

As we have seen, the Pastorals urge a way of life which is

---

[1] Dibelius–Conzelmann, Introduction. This commentary stands within the tradition of German scholarship which spoke of the emergence of 'early catholicism' as the eschatological expectation of the Parousia faded and the church settled down in the world and became institutionalised. This approach located the Johannine epistles in the struggle between charismatic and institutionalised forms of Christianity, and the Pastorals were taken to represent the latter (see J. D. G. Dunn, *Unity and Diversity in the New Testament* (London, 1977), chapter 14). The notion of 'early catholicism' is thus connected with Dibelius' picture of 'bourgeois Christianity' noted in chapter 2, against which recent work has reacted: R. Schwartz, *Bürgerliches Christentum im Neuen Testament? Österreichische Biblische Studien* 4 (Klosterneuburg, 1983); Towner, *The Goal of our Instruction*; Kidd, *Wealth and Beneficence*.

grounded in a particular theological view of the way the world is. That view reinforces a positive acceptance of the created order and of society as established by God. It tends against radicalism, and towards the maintenance of social hierarchy. But that is not to say that the result is a kind of primitive catholic orthodoxy. Certainly the stance and language of the Pastorals, read in a particular way when these letters reached canonical status, reinforced the doctrinal authority structures of the church. Certainly there is emphasis on a tradition inherited from Paul, focussed perhaps in the 'faithful sayings', as 'slogans' to be taught, memorised and passed on as safe-guards against false teaching. Nevertheless it is important to set this insistence on 'sound teaching' in its appropriate social context, and avoid projecting back those notions of 'doctrine' and 'orthodoxy' which emerged in the course of time.

THE IMPORTANCE OF TEACHING IN THE PASTORALS

Didaskalia, the Greek word for 'teaching', occurs fifteen times in these three little letters, over against six in the whole of the rest of the New Testament. The urgency that church officials be *didaktikoi*, 'apt for teaching', appears twice, and nowhere else in the New Testament. Uniquely, too, Paul is twice described as a *didaskalos*, or 'teacher', alongside the usual *apostolos*. The noun *didachē* and the verb *didaskō*, in both simple and compound forms, punctuate the text, but their frequency elsewhere in the New Testament makes their use less dramati-cally striking. Other associated words for advising, exhorting, directing, commanding, etc. permeate the letters.

It has been remarked that *pistis* is used in the Pastorals to refer to 'the faith' or, we might say, 'Christianity'; but if anything the use of *didaskalia* in this kind of way is even more striking. But of course there is also the opposite, the 'teaching of the demons', or the activity of *heterodidaskalein*, 'teaching other-wise' than these letters approve, a word apparently coined by the author of these texts, found twice in 1 Timothy but other-wise unknown except in later Christian texts. The problems occasioning these letters relate to teaching. The response to the situation produces an emphasis on teaching that which is approved.

Let us consider a few key passages:

1 Timothy 4.6

Timothy is told that, by setting the foregoing advice before the brethren, he will demonstrate that he is a good servant of Christ Jesus, and that he himself is nurtured or trained in the words of the faith and of the good teaching (in both cases, the word for 'good' is *kalos*, 'fine' or 'noble') which he has followed.

1 Timothy 4.12–13 and 16

Timothy is told to be a 'type' or example for believers in speech and behaviour, love, faith (or fidelity) and purity. He is to devote himself to reading, exhortation and teaching. He is to take pains with himself and the teaching.

1 Timothy 5.17

Those presbyters who work hard at preaching and teaching are to get special recognition.

1 Timothy 6.1

Slaves are to respect their masters so that the teaching is not brought into disrepute.

1 Timothy 6.2b–3

Timothy is told to teach and preach what has been presented earlier in the text, and anyone teaching anything else without attending to the 'healthy' words of our Lord Jesus Christ and the teaching which is in accord with *eusebeia*, piety or godliness, is treated as unworthy of attention – puffed up, lacking in understanding, diseased with speculations and disputes, inspiring envy, strife, blasphemy, wicked ideas, irritation, etc.

2 Timothy 3.10–16

Timothy has followed Paul's teaching and manner of life, his resolution, faithfulness, patience, love, and fortitude under persecution and suffering. Everyone who wants to live with piety (*eusebōs*) in Christ Jesus will be persecuted. But Timothy is to stand by what he has learnt, knowing from whom he has learnt it. He is to remember that he has known the scriptures, the 'holy writings', since childhood, and that these are able to make him wise for salvation through faith in Jesus Christ. Every written text that is inspired is also profitable for teaching, for correction, for reformation, for training in righteousness.

2 Timothy 4.3

The time is coming, we are told, when people will not tolerate 'healthy teaching', but according to their own private inclinations, will gather teachers who tickle their ears, and they will switch their hearing away from truth and turn to fables.

Titus 1.7–9

The bishop is to have the qualities which will make him hold fast to the trustworthy word which accords with the *didachē*, that he may be able to exhort in the 'healthy teaching' (*didaskalia*) and refute objectors.

Titus 2.1

Titus is to speak what befits the 'healthy teaching'.

Titus 2.7

In exhorting younger people to behave temperately, Titus is to set an example (*typos*) of good works. In his teaching, he is to demonstrate integrity and seriousness, providing a 'healthy word' which is beyond reproach.

Titus 2.10

Slaves are to behave so that they 'adorn' or perhaps 'do credit
to', the teaching of our Saviour God *en pasin*, either 'in every
way' or 'amongst everyone'.

These passages are far from exhausting the relevant material. As we have already noted, the bulk of these letters is
paraenesis, ethical advice and exhortation, teaching, in other
words. The fact that there are something like seventy impera-
tives indicates the didactic tone; another twenty-five indirect
expressions of command or expectation reinforce the impression. The purpose for which Timothy and Titus are delegated
is to 'instruct' (*parangellō, parangelia*) or to 'exhort' (*parakaleō,
paraklēsis*, words which mean something like 'appeal' or
'encourage', but with some authority behind the moral
pressure!). Such vocabulary occurs at the rate of about ten
times each root. In 1 Timothy 1.5 it is insisted that 'love is the
aim of the instruction' (*parangelia*), but love does not exclude
reproof or prescription: 'these are the themes, the exhortations,
the reproofs you must offer with all command; let no-one
disregard you' (Titus 2.15), and this is not the only occasion
when such strong language is used.

Teachers need learners, and the verb 'to learn' (*manthanō*)
occurs six times (though not the noun *mathētēs* ('disciple'),
which interestingly does not occur outside the gospels and
Acts); more common are words implying subordination or lack
of it (three of the four New Testament occurrences of *anupotak-
tos* are found in the Pastorals). Obedience is enjoined and
expected, except of the disruptive false teachers whose lack of
obedience is the fundamental problem.

A number of times 'training' (*paideia, paideuein*) is referred to,
twice through discipline, as when Hymenaeus and Alexander
are consigned to Satan so that they may learn (*paideuthōsin* –
'be trained' or 'educated') not to blaspheme (1 Tim. 1.20); and
when the 'slave of God' is told not to be quarrelsome, but
gentle in 'training' or 'disciplining' those who oppose him (2
Tim. 2.25). In Titus 2.11, God's grace is described as 'training'

us to renounce godless ways and worldly desires and to live with temperance, justice and piety in the present age. Most important of all, Timothy's own education in the scriptures is recalled as the usefulness of every inspired written text for teaching, reproof, reformation and 'training' in righteousness is affirmed. Metaphors of athletic training also punctuate the letters: training for the body (*gymnasia*) is of limited benefit compared with stripping for *eusebeia*, or the practice of piety (1 Tim. 4.7–8); the man of God is to run the great race of faith, as the usual translations put it, but the Greek refers to struggling in any athletic contest, even a wrestling-match.

The training and teaching by which these letters set so much store appears to be the instruction in moral behaviour and proper relationships within the church which constitutes the content of these epistles. Much depends on the character of office-holders who are to set an example. Even though women are not allowed to teach or dictate to men but should keep quiet, according to 1 Tim. 2.12, in Titus 2.3ff. older women are specifically charged with setting an example, with being *kalodidaskaloi*, a word found nowhere else and meaning 'teaching what is good', so as to advise and direct younger women. Exemplary conduct and instruction are envisaged as proceeding from the top down, and those who learn are subject to authority. It is important to set this in its cultural context before we consider its bearing on the nature of the 'doctrine' in these epistles.

TEACHING AND LEARNING IN THE ANCIENT WORLD

The education of mind and body through *paideia* was the classical Greek ideal,[2] which makes the metaphorical association of physical and spiritual training in the Pastorals of

[2] For the impact of the gymnasium (the centre of Hellenic physical and mental culture) on Jews, see V. Tcherikover, *Hellenistic Civilisation and the Jews*, ET S. Appelbaum (Philadelphia, 1959). Werner Jaeger, *Paideia: The Ideals of Greek Culture*, ET Gilbert Highet (3 vols., Oxford, 1943–5), is a classic study of competing educational ideals in the classical tradition; he followed this with *Early Christianity and Greek Paideia* (Cambridge, MA, 1961). See also H. I. Marrou, *A History of Education in Antiquity*, ET George Lamb (London, 1956).

particular interest. Under the influence of Greek ideals of *paideia*, the Greco-Roman world was self-conscious about its educational processes, and the Pastorals reflect that world and its culture. Literature formed the basis of education, and was the principal medium whereby 'Hellenisation' was effectively disseminated, urban societies being shaped by the dominant ethos.[3] High value was placed on books, and on the ancient wisdom of the classical literature.[4]

In practice access to education tended to be for the elite, and the extent of literacy has been often overestimated.[5] The bulk of the population, peasants, artisans, slaves, women, had little access to schooling and little use for reading or writing. However, by the Hellenistic and Roman periods, the use of writing was widespread in urban society. Even those who may not themselves have been literate made use of literacy in legal and business transactions, if only through the medium of professional scribes or slaves trained to be literate; larger businesses and the imperial bureaucracy demanded record-keeping. It would be a disgrace for an upper-class man to be illiterate, even though he would own or employ secretaries or copyists to do most of his writing.

Literary culture, then, was generally the preserve of the leisured elite, but books had a kind of mystique. Within the closely packed urban setting, there was what we might call a 'filter-down' effect, through public oratory, theatre, etc. We have to imagine a society in which, at least for men, life was lived in public and to a fair extent in the open air. The oral medium remained important, many small businesses relying on word of mouth, popular philosophical teachers discoursing in the public porticoes, and so on. Indeed, even literature remained oral in the sense that it was always treated like a

---

[3] A. H. M. Jones, *The Greek City from Alexander to Justinian* (Oxford, 1940).

[4] On books in the ancient world, see three articles by C. H. Roberts, 'The Codex', in *Proceedings of the British Academy* (1954); 'Books in the Graeco-Roman World and in the New Testament', in *The Cambridge History of the Bible*, ed. P. R. Ackroyd and C. F. Evans (Cambridge, 1970); 'The Writing and Dissemination of Literature in the Classical World', chapter 19 of *Literature and Western Civilisation*, vol. i, ed. David Daiches (London, 1972).

[5] William V. Harris, *Ancient Literacy* (Cambridge, MA, 1989).

tape, a way of recording so as to replay the spoken word, reading was always aloud, even in private, and texts were memorised.[6] But still we are speaking of a culture in which book learning was valued, and respected even by those who had little direct access to it.

In various ways, Jews were affected by this Hellenistic context, and, it seems, both participated in the local Greek schools and through their synagogue schools gave their offspring training in their own alternative literature, the scriptures. When, as already noted, the Pastoral epistles show the early Christian community as one that also valued book learning, stating that *graphē*, written material, is inspired and useful for teaching and training (2 Tim. 3.16), without doubt the literary legacy received by Christians from the Jews is referred to, but the point is that the Jewish reverence for the written Word of God reinforces a pervasive cultural pattern.

But if we are to understand the emphasis on teaching in the Pastoral epistles, we also have to look at contexts other than schools, where, as we have seen, the participation rate is unlikely to have been high in terms of the whole of society. We have to understand that ancient society was structured very differently from modern societies. As E. A. Judge put it, 'the political competition was not conducted between economic strata horizontally organised [by which he refers to the 'class struggle'], but between vertically organised social hierarchies'.[7] The local aristocracy consisted of property-owners who were heads of households, and most of the rest of society were in some sense dependants or 'hangers-on'. Not only were servants, slaves, ex-slaves, employees, tenants and others beholden to the household head, but the system of patronage whereby an influential person had obligations 'to protect the economic and legal interests of clients' and the clients therefore to accept their subordination and offer their support to the patron means that

[6] George A. Kennedy, *Classical Rhetoric and its Christian and Secular Tradition from Ancient to Modern Times* (California and London, 1980), pp. 109ff.: 'The introduction of writing into Greece tended to freeze speech into texts.'

[7] E. A. Judge, 'The Early Christians as a Scholastic Community', *Journal of Religious History*, 1 (1960–1), 6–7.

our concepts of class are inappropriate for understanding societal relationships in the ancient world.[8] In such a society, Judge suggests, philosophical ideas did not circulate widely through 'the formal tradition of the great classical schools', or through street preachers, but through the talk that took place in household communities.

Indeed, it was in the household that much education and training must have taken place. The head of the household was responsible for the appropriate nurture of family and servants. The master might send certain slaves to school to acquire skills appropriate to future functions in the household or its business. The father, with the mother, was responsible for the education of children up to the age at which it was felt appropriate to send each child with a *paidagōgus*, the attendant slave, to further education with the *grammaticus* and *rhētor*. The extent to which girls were given schooling is debated, but certainly there were literate matrons in high-class households, and both the education of young children and the training of the women, whether daughters or servants, was the responsibility of the wife of the head of the household.

The household was structured hierarchically, and both by example and precept the higher ranks taught the lower ranks. No doubt a servant or slave picked up necessary practical skills by being apprenticed to other servants or slaves, but the general ethos of the household, its relationships and obligations, was set by the patriarch. In popular moral philosophy, as we have seen, a standard *topos* concerned household management and the duties built into the relationship of husband and wife, father and child, master and slave.[9] Since each household was regarded as a little state, the proper ordering of households ensured the proper ordering of society. Conversely a good king or ruler set an example for those who ruled households. Discipline and proper honour, respect, subordination, obedience, were keys to instruction, though much instruction implied imitation of the example set by one's super-

[8] E. A. Judge, 'St. Paul and Classical Society', *Jahrbuch für Antike und Christentum* 15 (1972), 19–36.
[9] See further Verner, *The Household of God*.

iors. To fulfil their teaching obligation, however, both rulers and masters of households might employ a kind of philosopher-chaplain to guide their own lives and to see that proper training for life through ethical precept was offered to the society over which they presided.

We are observing a society in which there was a fascination with instruction and with ethical questions, and where, even though few would attend philosophical schools, many set themselves up as travelling philosophers offering teaching about life and proper conduct. Such teachers, wearing the well-known mantle, were familiar figures in street and household. That Paul would have been recognised as such a teacher, and that the church was a kind of philosophical school based in local households, has been cogently argued by a number of recent scholars. This is the social background of the Pastorals and its interest in teaching.

In these letters, there is no dwelling upon credal orthodoxy, and, I would suggest, few hints of the imposition of *belief* by episcopal authority, except in so far as heresy is to be avoided and the tradition maintained.[10] Rather the predominant concern is about correct relationships, duties and obligations in a community which regards itself as a teaching environment with a pattern of virtuous behaviour and a set of authoritative writings. These writings had been adopted from the Jews, who met regularly to read and learn from them in their synagogues, a habit also inherited and adapted to Christian purposes. Now, 'the main object of these Sabbath meetings was not religious worship in the narrower sense, but religious teaching, i.e. instruction in the Torah'; so Philo is 'not far wrong when he calls synagogues schools (*didaskaleia*)', describing them as places 'where "the ancestral philosophy" was cultivated and every kind of virtue taught'.[11] For Jews the meaning of scrip-

---

[10] See chapters 3 and 6. Those who espouse the view that the Pastorals represent 'early catholicism' also suggest that *pistis* has lost its Pauline force and become more credal in its sense. See TDNT and Towner, *The Goal of our Instruction*, pp. 121ff.

[11] The new Schürer, *The History of the Jewish People in the Age of Jesus Christ*, vol. II, revised and edited by Geza Vermes, Fergus Millar and Matthew Black (Edinburgh, 1979), pp. 424–5.

ture was Halakah, instruction in the way of life. Indeed, those adopted scriptures themselves reinforced in their proverbs and law-codes the notion of passing on a stable world by living according to divine precepts. The traditions of biblical wisdom encouraged respect for seniors, discipline of children, continuity, honest dealing, and the basic values of a recognisably universal social ethic. So it is hardly surprising that the communities of the Pastorals saw scriptural teaching about the Christian way in ethical terms, and the primary function of the church as teaching. The universal God had revealed 'sound teaching' about the proper way of life.

THE PASTORALS AND THE POPULAR PHILOSOPHERS

The work of E. A. Judge first drew attention to the important analogies between the early church and what he called a 'scholastic community', and his work was developed by Abraham Malherbe.[12] Despite the importance of other analogies, such as the household and the association (*koinōnia*), it is worth pursuing this a bit further to understand the Pastorals.

Judge designated Paul a 'sophist', a term 'chosen for lack of a better',[13] and defined by Judge as including philosophers as well as orators. Paul's travelling and preaching behaviour, in his view, provokes this parallel. He was sponsored by about forty patrons, and another forty or so persons can be identified among his professional following. Judge believes, then, that 'local notabilities' sponsored Paul – indeed 'Christian groups rested for their security on the maintenance of some sort of social hierarchy under whose auspices they met.' He argues that Paul turned to this new profession when his old one of rabbi failed and he was excluded from the synagogues.

Paul, Judge notes, 'is always anxious about the transmission of the *logos* and the acquisition of *gnōsis* ... The Christian faith, therefore, as Paul expounds it, belongs with the doctrines of the

---

[12] Judge, 'St. Paul and Classical Society', and *The Social Pattern of Christian Groups in the First Century* (London, 1960). Abraham J. Malherbe, *Social Aspects of Early Christianity*, 2nd enlarged edition (Philadelphia, 1983); *Paul and the Popular Philosophers.*
[13] Judge, 'The Early Christians as a Scholastic Community'.

philosophical schools rather than with the esoteric rituals of the mystery religions' (pp. 135ff.).[14] In developing his thesis, Judge further notes that Paul attacks his opponents on questions of belief and moral practice, and cultic or religious activities as they would be recognised in the ancient world are not a matter of concern. There are unusual features: 'What other touring preacher established a set of corporate societies independent of himself yet linked to him by a constant traffic of delegations?' Yet Paul also denounces his opponents in terms which are recognisable as typical of controversy between popular philosophers.

It is this latter element that Malherbe pursued. In his work on Thessalonians, he demonstrated the Cynic background to Paul's language of apology and attack.[15] Drawing on the works of Dio Chrysostom (AD 40–c. 120), he shows how a philosopher-preacher would defend and characterise himself, distinguishing himself from sophists and rhetoricians, and from other philosophical types. From this emerges a picture of a variety of ways in which so-called philosophers operated and were perceived. Here we meet the street-preachers, the resident philosophers and those holding forth in lecture-rooms, and also an attempt to delineate the 'true philosopher'.

The true philosopher conceived it as his right and duty to speak out with *parrhēsia* ('freedom', 'boldness'), and act as example because of his *philanthrōpia*, his love for humanity. It

---

[14] In normal everyday parlance, the Greek word *logos*, it should be noted, simply means 'discourse' and the word *gnōsis* just means 'knowledge'; in other words, they are the stuff of an education that set much store by language and wisdom, and do not necessarily imply more exotic gnostic ideas.

[15] 'Cynics differed among themselves in their philosophical eclecticism ... What made a Cynic was his dress and conduct, self-sufficiency, harsh behaviour towards what appeared as excesses, and a practical ethical idealism ... The resulting diversity makes an attempt at a detailed definition of Cynicism difficult.' So Malherbe in 'Self-definition among the Cynics', in *Jewish and Christian Self-Definition*, vol. 3, *Self-Definition in the Greco-Roman World*, ed. B. F. Meyer and E. P. Sanders (London, 1982). Cynics were philosophers who 'freed' themselves of the normal social constraints; for a challenging popular presentation of their style and similarity to Jesus, see F. Gerald Downing, *Jesus and the Threat of Freedom* (London, 1987). For Malherbe's work on the Pauline material, see '"Gentle as a Nurse"', and 'Exhortation in I Thessalonians', *Novum Testamentum* 25 (1983), 238–56, both reprinted in *Paul and the Popular Philosophers*. See also *Paul and the Thessalonians: The Philosophic Tradition of Pastoral Care* (Philadelphia, 1987).

was necessary to be harsh and critical for the good of all people when appropriate. Even when scorned and rejected, such a Cynic will persist 'with gentle words at times, at others harsh'.[16] So the Cynics' reputation for 'hatred of mankind' was countered by a stress on the fact that the true philosophers had understanding of human nature, and distinctions were drawn between admonition and reproach, one being gentle, the other objectionable, one correcting, the other merely reproving. The figure of the nurse appears, as one who both disciplines and comforts. Malherbe sums up: '*Parrhēsia*, like other medicine, must be applied properly.'[17] The ideal philosopher

who with purity and without guile speaks with a philosopher's boldness, not for the sake of glory, nor making false pretensions for the sake of gain, who stands ready out of good will and concern for his fellowman, if need be, to submit to ridicule

is not easily found, and Dio adds

in my own case I feel that I have chosen that role, not of my own volition, but by the will of some deity. For when divine providence is at work for men, the gods provide, not only good counsellors who need no urging, but also words that are appropriate and profitable to the listener.[18]

Malherbe proceeds to draw out the many parallels between Dio's language and that of Paul. But our concern is not immediately with Paul, significant as it is that his converts would have judged him according to these categories; rather it is with Malherbe's development of these themes in relation to the Pastoral epistles.

Malherbe devotes one of his articles to exploring the parallels between the language of teaching and polemic in the Pastorals and the kind of material to which attention has

---

[16] Dio Chrysostom, *Discourses* 77/78.38, quoted by Malherbe, *Paul and the Popular Philosophers*, p. 41.

[17] Referring to Plutarch, *How to Tell a Flatterer from a Friend* 68A–70D, quoted by Malherbe, *Paul and the Popular Philosophers*, p. 45.

[18] Dio Chrysostom, *Discourses* 32.11–12, quoted by Malherbe, *Paul and the Popular Philosophers*, pp.45–6.

already been drawn.[19] 'The description of human vices and passions as diseases was widespread, but was especially used by Stoics and Cynics',[20] and so the idea that 'healthy' or 'sound' teaching was needed to cure moral ills was natural, and the philosopher was regarded as the physician of the soul. Dio Chrysostom again provides contemporary examples.

The picture of the Cynics which emerges from the sources shows them challenging the established education of the Greek world as inadequate medicine, and prescribing severe treatment for the corrupt human condition. They were controversial figures, often opposed and satirised, and so other philosophers distanced themselves from them, accusing them of being diseased themselves, and causing contention and therefore further disease. 'The use of the medical imagery in the Pastorals is thoroughly polemical', concludes Malherbe. By contrast, the 'orthodox teacher' is 'gentle and mild, knowing when to be severe, concerned with personal moral progress', one 'who preaches to benefit others', and one 'who promotes social stability' – a figure indeed comparable to Dio's ideal philosopher and the 'antithesis to misanthropic, antisocial Cynics'.[21]

To Malherbe's material we may add another significant point to which MacDonald draws attention.[22] The depiction of Paul in the legends of the apocryphal Acts is exactly like the popular view of the anti-social Cynic: wandering from city to city, eschewing marriage and civic commitments, an indigent itinerant, preaching a morality opposed to the dominant society.

---

[19] 'Medical Imagery in the Pastoral Epistles', first published in *Texts and Testaments: Critical Essays on the Bible and Early Christian Fathers*, ed. W. E. March (San Antonio, TX, 1980), reprinted as chapter 8, pp. 121–36, in Malherbe, *Paul and the Popular Philosophers*. See also '"In Season and out of Season": 2 Timothy 4.2', first published in *JBL* 103 (1984), 235–43, and reprinted as chapter 9, pp. 137–45, in Malherbe, *Paul and the Popular Philosophers*.

[20] Malherbe, *Paul and the Popular Philosophers*, p. 127.   [21] *Ibid.*, p. 136.

[22] MacDonald, *The Legend and the Apostle*, p. 47. Cf. the association of Christians with Cynics in Aelius Aristides, *ibid.*, p. 46, quoted above, chapter 1. Here MacDonald notes the evidence that the early Christians invited the charge of social marginality by regarding themselves as 'aliens' and 'sojourners', citizens of heaven, and the concern of the Apologists to meet this charge. The Pastorals anticipate this need.

Altogether, this background illuminates both the central importance of ethical teaching, and the way in which 'sound doctrine' functions polemically against the false teachers. Those who used these letters presented Paul as a moral teacher, and his legacy, based on received wisdom found in scripture, as 'sound teaching' which upheld social convention rather than undermining it. Like the Cynics, the false teachers were uncomfortable subversives. The fundamental issue between these letters and those they oppose concerns the proper interpretation of the life and teaching of Paul.

LEARNING BY EXAMPLE, INSTRUCTION AND 'PARAENESIS'

The importance of imitation for the development of moral character in the perception of the ancient world can hardly be overestimated.[23] Regularly the theme appears in treatment of the father–son relationship, young men being exhorted to pattern their lives after their fathers, and fathers to set a proper example. It is also used of the relation of subjects and rulers, who were ideally expected to set forth a perfect model of virtue. Pupils, too, were expected to imitate their teachers, both in behaviour and practice, and a good teacher was regarded as far better than books. The good, too, were to be imitated, not just praised.

Cherish some man of high character, and keep him ever before your eyes, living as if he were watching you, and ordering all your actions as if he beheld them ... The soul should have someone to respect – one by whose authority it may make even its inner shrine more hallowed. Happy is the man who can make others better, not merely when he is in their company, but even when he is in their thoughts! ... Choose a master whose life, conversation, and soul-expressing face have satisfied you; picture him always to yourself as your protector and your pattern. For we must indeed have someone according to whom we may regulate our characters ...[24]

---

[23] See Ernest Best, *Paul and his Converts* (Edinburgh, 1988), pp. 60–3. The theme is treated more fully, it seems, by B. Fiore, *The Function of Personal Example in the Socratic and Pastoral Epistles*, Analecta Biblica (Rome, 1986), but I have been unable to obtain this work.

[24] Seneca, *Epistles* 11.8–10.

The passage comes from the Roman moralist of Stoic[25] persuasion, Seneca, who was a kind of imperial chaplain, but also a man recognised later by Christians as 'frequently our own', so much so that a correspondence between Paul and Seneca appears among the New Testament apocrypha.[26] Malherbe[27] quotes the passage to draw out further similarities between Paul and those philosophers who claimed to do people good. The importance of exemplary behaviour and imitation of a moral hero was recognised, and Paul's references to himself as an example his converts followed, or should follow, are comparatively frequent.

In the Pastorals, Paul continues to play that role, but it is also clear that exemplary behaviour is built into the sound teaching which Christians are expected to follow at every level. The household of God is a teaching and learning community. It is time to look again at the contents of these epistles in the light of the background we have been tracing.

Paul is presented as an instructor, a *didaskalos* (1 Tim. 2.7), and the content of the letters rehearses his instruction. Timothy and Titus are to be instructors like Paul. They are charged with the task of teaching proper conduct to the household of God. Their own conduct is to be exemplary (1 Tim. 4.12; Titus 2.7), but they are also to engage in critical admonition for the good of the community, like the ideal philosopher, and unlike the false teachers who do not have love, or truth, as their principal objective. Such people are like the false philosophers who disrupt society or teach for personal gain.

The context of the teaching and admonition is the household of God. The metaphor suggests that God is the head of the household, the *episkopos* is the head-steward or administrator,

---

[25] Stoicism was the philosophical position adopted by a majority of influential Romans in the first centuries BC-AD. It placed a great deal of emphasis on ethics, and tended to identify 'nature' with the divine. Living 'according to nature' meant in accordance with the divine Logos which was the rationality permeating everything. See J. M. Rist, *Stoic Philosophy* (Cambridge, 1969).

[26] Hennecke, *New Testament Apocrypha*, vol. II, pp. 133ff.

[27] In another article republished in *Paul and the Popular Philosophers*, as chapter 5, pp. 67–77, 'Paul: Hellenistic Philosopher or Christian Pastor?', originally in *Anglican Theological Review* 68 (1986), 3–13.

and Timothy or Titus are the 'philosopher-chaplains' who represent Paul, passing on his teaching and moral advice. The teaching is codified according to accepted conventions, and largely consists of delineations of virtuous character and appropriate behaviour, expressed in proper relations between different grades in the hierarchy of the household. Such moral advice and such a perception of the principal focus of the Christian message are also found in the so-called Apostolic Fathers, where ethics and admonition express the way of life revealed by Christ as being the will of God.

Inherent in all this is a perception that proper relations reflect a hierarchy, like the hierarchies of the many parallel households which made up society. The hierarchy in the Pastorals would appear to be God, Christ, Paul, Timothy, head-steward (bishop), seniors (presbyters), servants (deacons), women, children, slaves, though the details will need reconsideration later. The point here is that the hierarchy of service reflected the way in which the master of the household (God) entrusted his business and his authority to his underlings. Instruction came from God via his ambassador, the sophist-teacher, Paul, then via Paul's delegates, to be invested in the ordered structure of the church. So we find that the very essence of the teaching is conveyed by the relationships and ethical values passed on in these epistles. We are not yet dealing with a conflict between orthodox belief and a rival creed. We are dealing with training in the duties and obligations of the Christian religion. These may be given theological sanction, or indeed scriptural warrant. But it is not surprising that the epistles demonstrate no doctrinal argument beyond the theological assertions explored in the last chapter. What is important is exemplary conduct and appropriate admonition to a God-ordained lifestyle.

And the same is true, within the hierarchy, for women. As the hierarchical order means that the head of household is not just apex but example to all lower ranks, so there are hierarchical relationships among the women of the household, and women should both set an example to and teach the women lower down the hierarchy. Older women, as well as men, are to receive respect (1 Tim. 5.1–2); and women enrolled as widows must be worthy of respect, having gained a reputation for good deeds, and their exemplary conduct is spelt out in terms of taking care of children, showing hospitality, washing the feet of God's people and supporting those in distress (1 Tim. 5.9–10). Older men should be sober, dignified, temperate, and sound in faith, love and fortitude; and older women similarly should be reverent in their demeanour, not scandal-mongers or slaves to excessive drinking, but setting a high standard so as to teach the younger women to be loving wives and mothers, to be temperate, chaste, busy at home, kind and respectful of their husband's authority (Titus 2.3–4).

As noted in chapter 1, recent studies have strongly suggested that it was teaching which subverted the proper hierarchy of the household that occasioned these letters, and particularly teaching which led to what was perceived as misbehaviour among women. It is interesting to note that 1 Clement is addressed to a rather similar situation, though here it seems to be the young men rather than the women who are causing disruption. The letter bemoans what has happened in the light of their previous sober piety, characterising it in terms of the domestic virtues of hospitality, and the instruction of the young and of women in obedience and propriety. Humble-mindedness had produced peace and goodness. But now through jealousy and strife, all these virtues are lost, and the letter is a call to obedience to God's commandments, and the order God established in the church. Each is to be well-pleasing to God in his own rank, with a good conscience, not transgressing the rule laid down for his office. A bishop is not to be removed from his ministry. Love and obedience are the prime virtues. It is in this context that the emphasis on teaching and listening, submitting and exhorting, exemplifying and imitating is to be understood.

OBEDIENCE

Pre-modern societies were built on structures of obligation, duty and obedience. The subordination of women in the

Pastoral epistles is part of a concept of society in which everyone is subordinate to someone, and even the ruler was understood to be subordinate to God. Bruce Malina's description[28] of the 'dyadic personality', though perhaps overdrawn in its contrasts, helps to delineate a shift of attitude in modern societies which explains our difficulties with much of the material we have been discussing.

In the social world of the New Testament, indeed of the Bible as a whole, honour and shame were pivotal values. The sort of personality such a culture fosters is one who sees himself or herself through the eyes of others. Reputation, or 'glory', is all important. Such a person needs others 'for any sort of meaningful existence, since the image he has of himself has to be indistinguishable from the image of himself held and presented to him by significant others in the family, village, city or nation' (p. 51). *Syneidēsis* (Greek) and *conscientia* (Latin, from which our 'conscience' is derived) literally meant 'with-knowledge', Malina notes; 'a person with conscience is a respectable, reputable, honourable person', someone sensitive to his public image, someone who has internalised what society expects of him. Malina points out there are no agonising psychological discussions of personal identity in ancient texts, no subtle explorations of motivation – indeed, prior to Augustine, no autobiographies. Our concept of the 'individual' is radically different from anything found in ancient literature. The first-century person saw the self in terms of structured relationships which both offered benefits and imposed obligations, the fulfilment of which would bring the honour sought, whereas non-fulfilment would be attended by shame and disgrace.

The discussion of ethical norms largely bears this out. Teaching was concerned with delineating the duties and obligations of one toward another, learning meant internalising these norms and copying those who exemplified them. The hierarchical structure of society meant that it was all the more important for those with authority and power to be themselves

[28] Malina, *The New Testament World*, especially chapter 3.

subject to moral constraint; the potential for petty tyranny was clearly enormous. But someone with authority and power who did not exercise it paternalistically would not gain a good reputation. The law of reciprocity in benefit and honour explored earlier tied the strata of the community to one another. Everyone, except those who kicked over the traces, was under constraint, whether they were high up on the status ladder or not.

Such values fostered an acceptance of obedience, whether to higher authority in the community or to traditional standards or to divine precepts. The extent to which the false teachers are both insubordinate and encourage insubordination in their hearers is a significant element in the situation and in the theological response of these letters.

Earlier, in referring to 2 Tim. 2.24, the English phrase 'slave of God' was used. Most translations prefer 'servant of God', but the term 'slave' was deliberately chosen. Paul had called himself a 'slave of Christ', and he retains that character in these epistles (Titus 1.1). Now slaves were to be obedient to their masters, and that directive is reinforced in these very letters. But obedience was compatible with exercising considerable freedom and authority. Studies of the institution of slavery in the ancient world have again alerted us to the problems of transposing our assumptions into a different social context.[29] Legally slaves were owned like property or animals, or indeed wives and children, and certainly slaves dreamed of freedom as an ultimate good. But there were slaves and slaves, and some legally 'free' persons would be no better, sometimes far worse off, often doing similar jobs for a pittance without the 'keep' a master was obliged to provide for his property. Not only were there manual labourers to work estates, mines and industries, not only were there domestic servants whose life as members of the family might not necessarily be hard or humiliating, but there were those slaves who were entrusted with major economic or political tasks by their masters, the managers of

---

[29] Dale B. Martin, *Slavery as Salvation: The Metaphor of Slavery in Pauline Christianity* (New Haven and London, 1990).

the estates, mines, industries or households, with powers of negotiation on their master's behalf, and invested with their master's authority. Being the slave of the right master could convey status.

So it was not humiliating for Paul to be called 'slave of Christ'. 'Slaves of Christ are those who represent Christ; they are active in the world as Christ's agents and wield his authority. Furthermore, it is expected that they will be rewarded with higher status, more authority, more power' (p. 55). But the term nevertheless implies a value-system in which obedience, indeed willing subservience, runs right through. In the Pastorals, teaching fosters that value-system. We should not underestimate the extent to which in his own writings Paul had expected obedience to himself, as 'father' of the churches he founded, and as Christ's ambassador-servant or slave.[30]

Yet Paul had spoken of exchanging for the spirit of slavery the spirit of sonship, of becoming children of God and therefore heirs with Christ, adopted sons rather than slaves (Rom. 8, especially). As I suggested above, the metaphor of the household is not worked out consistently, and a slave certainly lacked the status of members of the family, especially the son and heir. But the shift in the metaphor does not invalidate the general perspective, that learning obedience to master or father and subservience to the duties and obligations of one's position is perceived as virtue, especially when the Father or the Lord and Master is understood to be Christ or God himself. In the final chapter we shall have to consider the consequences of this analysis for our own appropriation of these texts. But the theology of the Pastorals unquestionably assumes that God is the apex of a hierarchically ordered society in which obedience is a prime value. The church is God's household, and he is King of the Universe. By God's grace and favour, Christians are members of his household, his 'slaves': so grace does not obviate obedience to God's instructions mediated through the household hierarchy.

---

[30] Best, *Paul and his Converts*, chapter 2; J. H. Schütz, *Paul and the Anatomy of Apostolic Authority* (Cambridge, 1975).

ORTHODOXY?

In the light of our explorations in this chapter, it must surely be clear that the 'doctrine' or 'teaching' of these epistles cannot be simplistically equated with orthodoxy as later understood. Indeed, the faith enjoined could well imply in many cases the faithfulness or fidelity of the obedient servant, rather than referring to any kind of credal or doctrinal beliefs. It is often linked with love, purity, good conscience (e.g. 1 Tim. 1.5, 19; 2.15; 3.9, etc.), and several times the adjective *anupokritos*, 'without pretence', is used to describe the kind of faith expected. This surely does not mean holding with sincerity to what became known as 'Christian dogma', but rather with an attitude of loyalty. The teaching is to do with lifestyle.

There are, however, two theological issues of some importance which are raised, and which we explored in earlier chapters, namely the goodness of creation and the appropriate place of the law. These discussions bear on the issue of ethics and lifestyle. The principal function of theological statements is to provide warrant for the ethical injunctions. They are introduced as well-known, common ground, and they provide a plausible belief-structure for the ethical teaching.

Are we to conclude then that the opposition was or was not promulgating alternative theological doctrines? Was the thing wrong with the false teaching simply its disruptive character, its challenge to the authority-structure? Such a perspective may well have a good deal in it, but there are features of the discussion which suggest that it may not be altogether adequate. Warrant for an ordered society rests in a shared assumption that God is the God of the universe, and that God has imparted his instructions to delegates who operate with his authority. Warrant for rejecting those authority-structures may well have been offered, on the one hand, by a view of the world as not originating from God's goodness, but as being a place from which the elect are alienated – in other words a form of gnosticism; and on the other hand, by a form of apocalyptic radicalism which consigned the present order to a phase soon to end, thus removing conventional constraints.

Warrant for the instruction offered is found in the sacred scriptures and the tradition of Paul's teaching. Warrant for alternative 'speculations' may well have been offered on the basis of the same written sources interpreted differently.

But if that is the case, only the authoritative hierarchically mediated tradition of 'sound teaching', the unquestionably 'right' hermeneutic, we might say, can effectively settle the argument – at least in the perspective represented in these epistles. They see no point in entering into a text-slinging match with those who claim to be *nomodidaskaloi*; but they will reinforce the authority of scripture by reference to Timothy's training in the sacred literature from his youth, and to its usefulness for instruction and reproof. They see no point in debating the false perspectives on creation and salvation offered by their rivals; but they will ram home the well-known slogans and doxologies and confessions of faith which carry the proper understanding of the tradition received in scripture and from Paul. The function of the 'faithful sayings', the words you can trust, is to provide the outlook on the world which will reinforce the teaching concerning the right way of life. These slogans bear the key to the appropriate interpretation of the Pauline tradition.

So is this appropriately designated 'early catholicism'? It certainly raises fundamental questions about the authority structures to be found in these epistles, questions about church order, the relative status of different groups or officers, and how authority is perceived. To these we will turn in the next chapter.

CHAPTER 5

Duties in the household of faith or What about church order?

The need for authority and discipline explored in the previous chapter has long been recognised as a feature of the Pastoral epistles. That required authority and discipline appears to be invested in a bishop, presbyters or elders, and deacons. Not surprisingly, therefore, the Pastorals have figured in debate about the nature of the church's order and ministry since the controversies of the Reformation, and more recent historical scholarship has been anxious to place the Pastorals' evidence within theories concerning the development of the ministry or priesthood of the church.[1] Here we have the terminology used which will become that of catholic orthodoxy. Hence the designation 'early catholicism'.

One problem is that because the terminology is used, it is far too easy to assume that 'bishop' means what a 'bishop' has become, that 'presbyters' are the 'priests' or 'elders' of later developments, and so on, projecting back anachronistic conceptions. This affects the perception not only of those who assume that these letters give scriptural authority for a particular form of ministry and therefore have a vested interest in showing that the Pastorals confirm that, but also of those engaged in historical research. A consensus has emerged that bishop and presbyters at this date overlapped, the bishop being

[1] H. von Campenhausen, *Ecclesiastical Authority and Spiritual Power in the Church of the First Three Centuries*, ET J. A. Baker (London, 1965); E. Schweizer, *Church Order in the New Testament*, ET F. Clarke (London, 1961). A convenient summary is found in J. D. G. Dunn, *Unity and Diversity in the New Testament* (London, 1977), pp.114–16. Most discussions of authorship note the problems of relating the church order implied by the Pastorals to the time of Paul: see commentaries.

simply the president of a college of elders; it is generally agreed
that only with Ignatius is the monepiscopate clearly established, and even then it could be argued that his insistence
reflects the need to recommend and defend an institution
which seems not yet to have won universal authority. More
recently, these letters have been used in arguments both for
and against women's ministry in the church.[2] All these debates,
I suggest, are conducted in terms of later perspectives.

What we need to do is to stretch our historical imaginations
and try to grasp what the original readers might have understood by the terms used: I shall avoid the usual terms in this
chapter, largely by retaining the Greek transliterated. We shall
apply the insights of recent sociological studies to these issues of
church order, building on what we have discovered before.

Three features of the text need to be noted, all arising from
the adaptation of household codes to a new ecclesiastical
context: (1) The so-called duty-codes are far more concerned
with moral qualities than functions; so it is hardly surprising
that what is said about *presbyteros* and *episkopos* overlaps – the
same qualities are also required of the *diakonoi*, and even
women. (2) The codes oscillate between seeing members of
God's household as servants or slaves under the direction of the
oikonomos, and as family members to be treated as father,
mother, brother, sister, presumably on the basis of Paul's claim
that converts are adopted and become sons and heirs in Christ.
(3) The codes vary in the extent to which they reflect an actual
household, speaking literally of the proper demeanour of old
and young, men and women, or slaves, and in the extent to
which the conventional form has been adapted to the church,
speaking metaphorically of ecclesiastical officers.

Thus the instructions to slaves appear to be giving literal
slaves the usual moral advice: they are to be submissive and

[2] Taken literally these epistles clearly subordinate women (see the discussion of 1 Tim.
2.9-15 in G. W. Knight's commentary), and reinforce the biblicist case against
women exercising roles of authority; but see Ben Witherington III, *Women in the
Earliest Churches*, SNTS Monograph Series 59 (Cambridge, 1988), pp. 117ff. for a
different exegesis. For the general issue, see Ruth B. Edwards, *The Case for Women's
Ministry* (London, 1989), pp. 8off. See below, pp. 113ff. and 114ff. for discussion of
women deacons and widows in the Pastorals.

obedient to their masters, to seek to please not contradict; they are not to pilfer but to demonstrate they are absolutely trustworthy (Titus 2.9–10); they must regard their masters as worthy of every honour – so those who have Christian masters must not presume on them simply because in Christ they are brothers (1 Tim. 6.1–2). It is not surprising, then, that other instructions (e.g. Titus 2.1–8) seem to be addressing members of the community simply as older and younger men, older and younger women: no church appointment is in view. This apparent confusion between two kinds of code leads to considerable ambiguity, which particularly affects the discussion of the *presbyteros* and the widow, but to some extent the *diakonos* and the *episkopos* as well. The explanation, I suggest, is that these texts reflect a process of transition, and the natural and technical use of a number of terms are not clearly distinguished. Even the *episkopos* and *diakonos* are in some sense still slaves functioning as servants in God's household.

It is important for a theology of the Pastorals to engage in this exploration. For theologically, the perspective of these letters appears to be that God's saving message has been entrusted to certain persons, and therefore the relationship to those persons and the tradition they carry is of eternal significance. Conversely, the behaviour of these persons is of inestimable importance for the validity of the gospel. We shall consider each office in turn.

THE 'EPISKOPOS'

As we might now expect, the texts tell us nothing about what the *episkopos* does. They are concerned that he be of a particular character. But those characteristics imply certain things.

According to 1 Tim. 3.2ff., the *episkopos* is to be *anepilēmptos*, 'irreproachable', a word unique to the New Testament, but common in other Greek texts of the period. It implies that his conduct is to bear public scrutiny and emerge unscathed. In assessing this term, it is worth recalling the description of an 'honour–shame' culture outlined in the last chapter. The *episkopos* is also to be *nephalios*, 'temperate in the use of wine', and *sōphrōn*, 'temperate and self-controlled' in all his behaviour. These virtues are classic for the Greek 'gentleman'[3] – one who was not able to restrain his own irrational desires was hardly a good example to others, or fit to lead and guide or have authority over others. Polycarp, in the letter to the Philippians which resembles the Pastorals so closely, makes that point explicit (11.2). These virtues are summed up in the next adjective, *kosmios*, 'respectable', 'honourable'. Further down the list (verse 3) we find this reinforced: the *episkopos* is not to be addicted to wine and quarrelsome, but reasonable and unaggressive, and not too fond of money. In other words, he has to have the character to be fair in his dealings with others. These are the qualities which bear comparison with those expected of the good general, as noted earlier in chapter 2.

That the *episkopos* should have such a character is clearly significant in terms of the social conformity of the community he leads and for which his behaviour is exemplary; no doubt it contrasts with the anti-social Cynic-type behaviour of the false teachers. Its moderation in all things may also contrast with the radical ascetic lifestyle others adopt. Meanwhile (verse 2), we are told that the *episkopos* should be *philoxenos*, 'hospitable', and *didaktikos*, 'apt for teaching'. The importance of 'teaching' to these communities has already been explored, and generally in early Christian texts, hospitality is highly valued, given the mobility and networking of those early communities, with their travelling apostles, prophets, etc.[4] The mention of hospitality reminds us, however, of the 'household' context, and the other characteristics spelt out here (verses 4–5) one might call 'domestic': he is to be the husband of one wife,[5] and to preside

---

[3] Dibelius–Conzelmann supply examples, ET p. 53.
[4] E.g. *Didachē* 11–13; 1 Clement 1, 10, 11, 12, etc. See *TDNT* – *xenos*, and Malherbe, *Social Aspects of Early Christianity*, pp. 66ff., and chapter 4 *passim*, especially pp. 98ff.
[5] The exact meaning of this is disputed. It seems unlikely that it simply enjoins monogamy, since that was the normal social situation. Avoidance of *porneia* would be a more natural way of enjoining abstention from sexual sin or adultery. It is most likely that it means being married only once, that is not remarrying if widowed or

with dignity over his own household, with his children subject to his authority – for if someone does not know how to preside over his own household, how can he have a proper care for the church of God? Similar comments are found in other Greek texts concerned with ethics: Dibelius–Conzelmann quote Isocrates,

Manage the city as you would your ancestral estate: in the matter of its appointments, spendidly and royally, in the matter of its revenues, strictly, in order that you may possess the good opinion of your people. (*Ad Nicoclem* 19)

All this suggests that the *episkopos* has a very considerable amount of authority, not unlike a head of household. But this household is not his own – it is God's (1 Tim. 3.15). So his position is not one of inheritance or right, but one of appointment. It would seem that some leading Christian householders may have assumed they should have the role by right, or that inappropriate ambition had fed those seeking such an appointment. For the very first statement in 1 Tim. 3.1b is 'if anyone aims at the episcopate, he desires to take upon himself a good work'. This kind of *kalon ergon* is analogous to the benefactions the richer citizens would make in service to their city, and the text is approving the willingness of property-owning Christians to serve their communities. In verses 6–7, however, we find the appointee is not to be a recent convert because the office might go to his head and he would find himself falling under the condemnation of the *diabolos*. That is generally assumed to be the devil in this Christian context, but the word means 'slanderer', and since the next verse refers to the need for a 'good testimony' from outsiders, one wonders whether the more general meaning is not more appropriate to the context.[6] So the office carried weight – people might seek it for the wrong ends – and the *episkopos* was in some sense the public face of the

divorced. Its importance as a quality of the *episkopos* could relate to extreme ascetic teachers suggesting marriage was in itself wrong.

6 Dibelius–Conzelmann, p. 54, excludes a 'slanderous person', and insists on 'devil' in both verse 6 and verse 7, as do most other commentators. But see Towner, *The Goal of our Instruction*, p. 230.

church, though he is not alone in being responsible for the impression created on non-Christians.[7]

In Titus 1.7ff., this material is repeated, with a combination of synonymous and overlapping terminology. Thus the *episkopos* is to be *anenklētos*, an alternative word for 'irreproachable'. He is not to be arrogant or self-willed, quick-tempered or addicted to wine, aggressive or grasping in a dishonest way. Rather he is to be hospitable, devoted to goodness, temperate in character, just, holy and self-restrained. He is also to be opposed to teaching which is contrary to the 'teaching of the word of faith'.[8] He is to be capable of exhorting and encouraging in the 'healthy teaching' and reproving those who contradict it. In Titus, then, the teaching function is given more prominence, the difficult context in which that teaching has to be offered being emphasised and further stated in the subsequent verses, but largely the passage repeats what has gone before.

Here, however, we find a particularly important clue to the status of the *episkopos*: he is described as *theou oikonomos*, 'God's steward'. In the last chapter we looked briefly at slavery in the world of antiquity. It is important to return to that discussion.[9] The majority of those slaves who were able to record their jobs on tombstones, dedications and honorary inscriptions were those who had administrative and managerial positions, and *oikonomos* is the term they generally used for themselves. An *oikonomos* worked as steward of a household or estate, or as business manager. He was probably literate and acted as secretary, record-keeper, treasurer or financial bursar. He might be the agent of a private person, or a public official like a city administrator, or even an imperial official (the civil service was known as Caesar's household – which should again alert us to the parallels between the theological vocabulary of these

---

[7] Even slaves have the responsibility of doing credit to Christian teaching: Titus 2. 9.

[8] *Tēn didachēn pistou logou*: literally, 'the teaching of the faithful word', which interestingly echoes the slogan, *Pistos ho logos* – 'Faithful is the saying', which punctuates these epistles. Presumably, however, it refers to the trustworthy gospel, and so might be translated as suggested.

[9] What follows is dependent on Martin, *Slavery as Salvation*, pp. 13–22, where many examples are offered.

letters and the ruler-cult[10]). Some *oikonomoi* were legally free and employed as servants, but many were slaves, and others were 'freedmen' or ex-slaves who had been granted or had earned manumission. Whatever their legal status, which made no difference to the job, they could have considerable power as agents empowered to act on the master's behalf. The owner's power and authority was vested in them, and yet they had freedom of manoeuvre, and some acquired private funds and business interests on the side.

The word *episkopos* itself simply meant someone who keeps an eye on things – it could even be used of God as the one who 'over-sees' the good and the bad; normally it referred to an 'overseer' or 'superintendent'. In putting the terminology together, it seems plausible to suggest that the household metaphor is of fundamental importance for understanding the duties of the *episkopos*. He is the one who is vested with God's authority to administer the church as God's household, to oversee the behaviour of the members of the household, to see that 'sound teaching' is promulgated, that proper order is maintained in gatherings for worship and in respectful, orderly interaction between members of the household community with different status and roles to perform. As a good steward, he stands for the head of the household, namely God, as Ignatius and the *Didascalia*[11] would suggest. Any authority he has is a delegated authority, but given its source, is it surprising that such a chief administrator rapidly acquired spiritual power over the rest of the community? The concern of the Pastorals is that the one appointed to that sort of place in the hierarchy should be a person with the appropriate character to set an example, to set the moral 'tone' of the community.

So we learn little about the actual duties placed upon this metaphorical head-steward, or the functions which he is expected to fulfil. But we do discover that he needs the qualities elsewhere required for the good general. That very metaphor is

---

[10] See chapter 3.
[11] Magnesians 6, Trallians 3, *Didascalia Apostolorum* ix (Syriac translated, with Latin fragments, by R. H. Connolly (Oxford, 1929), pp. 88–90).

found in 2 Tim. 2.3–4, and developed in 1 Clement in direct
application to the issue of authority in the church:

> Let us serve in our army, brethren, with all enthusiasm, following his
> [Christ's] faultless commands. Think of those who serve our [Roman]
> commanders in the field, with what good order, readiness and sub-
> missiveness they carry out their duties. Not all are marshalls, gen-
> erals, colonels, captains and so on, but each in his own rank carries
> out the orders given by king and commanders.[12]

To conclude, it is not yet clear that the *episkopos* has the kind
of authority acquired later, but given the structures and
assumptions of a hierarchically ordered society, the implication
is that he is 'the chief cook and bottle-washer', under the
authority of God. He is God's household manager, and the
reputation of the household depends upon his proper leadership and example. But the crucial question concerns his
relationship with the *presbyteroi*, and to that we now turn.

THE 'PRESBYTEROI'

As already noted, the majority view is that the *presbyteroi* and
episkopos are not clearly distinguished in the Pastorals. This
view is based chiefly on Titus 1.5–9. According to this text,
Titus was left in Crete in order to appoint *presbyteroi* in each
city, following Paul's directive. Anyone with the following
qualities would be appropriate: someone *anenklētos*, irreproachable, a husband of one wife, having faithful children not under
charge of dissipation or insubordination. The parallels with the
description of the *episkopos* are striking, and since this text goes
on, 'For the *episkopos* must be irreproachable', etc., many have
concluded that the characterising of an appropriate 'over-seer'
simply resumes the description of anyone fit to be a presbyter
and does not refer to a distinct office at all. This finds support
from the otherwise inexplicable omission of the *presbyteroi* from
the duty-code of 1 Tim. 3 – they must be there in the guise of
the *episkopos*. The fact that the word *episkopos* is consistently
found in the singular whereas the word *presbyteros* is usually in

[12] 1 Clement 37.

the plural form has led some to suggest that the singular *episkopos* is one of the presbyters who acts as president, or has the managerial duties of the presbyterate delegated to him.[13] The argument of this section is that this is not the most satisfactory reading of the Pastorals' evidence, and that a different perspective on the development of the presbyterate and a recognition of the transitional nature of the church at the time of these epistles may be significant for their self-understanding and their theological stance.

In 1 Tim. 3, an 'ecclesiastical' code speaks only of *episkopos* and *diakonoi*. The first appearance of a *presbyteros* comes much later, in chapter 5, and suggests no more than an older person with the status due to a senior citizen. Timothy is not to be harsh with a *presbyteros*, but appeal to him as he would his father, and he is to treat younger men as brothers (5.1). The familial metaphor is to the fore. The next verse refers to older women, who are to be treated as mothers, and younger women, who are to treated as sisters.

The same observation may be made about the information in Titus 2. Here old men, *presbyteis*, are told they should be *nephalioi*, 'temperate in the use of wine', *semnoi*, 'worthy of respect', *sōphrōnes*, 'temperate in behaviour and character', and healthy in faith, love and endurance. The next sentence turns to the qualities of old women, the subsequent one to those of young men. There is no doubt that it is simply the senior members of the community here referred to, and the qualities enjoined upon them overlap with those expected of the *episkopos* precisely because they, like him, should be setting a good example to everyone else, given their status and seniority.

In 1 Tim. 5.17, however, *presbyteroi* appear who, for performing well their functions of 'presiding', are to receive double pay. The word *timē* could simply mean 'honour', but reward for service was a way of marking 'honour', and in secular Greek the word could mean 'honorarium' or 'compensation' (in the New Testament it appears in the sense of 'price', e.g. Matt.

---

[13] For full discussion of these questions, see von Campenhausen, *Ecclesiastical Authority*. George W. Knight III, pp. 175ff., follows Lightfoot in regarding *presbyteros* and *episkopos* as synonyms. See also Kelly, pp. 13ff.; Hanson, pp. 31ff.; Houlden, pp. 73ff.

27.9); the matter has been disputed among commentators, but the following verses, where unusually for these epistles two 'texts' are quoted,[14] are strongly suggestive of monetary reward, especially for those who labour 'in the word and teaching', which, as we have seen, were matters of priority for these epistles. There seems little doubt, then, that we are now dealing with not just any older men, but certain senior men with a particular status in the community, and with functions valued by the community for which they receive monetary reward such as the apostles could claim. That the *presbyteroi* are likened to the Apostles in Ignatius and the *Didascalia* is intriguing in the light of this,[15] and a point to which we will return.

People who hold this position are not to be subject to arbitrary criticism: 'You should not receive a charge against a *presbyteros* without two or three witnesses' (5.19). This seems to presuppose that 'Timothy', or perhaps anyone who has inherited Paul's authority through Timothy, is in a position to deal with judicial charges even against *presbyteroi*, provision being made for formal charges only to be considered, not idle gossip.

'Those who persist in sin', we next read, are to be reproved in front of all, so that fear may restrain the rest (verse 20). Are these 'sinners' the defamators, or offending presbyters? And is the reproof in front of a constituted presbyterate or the whole community? Commentators tend to agree that the discipline of clergy is in view here,[16] but differ on the latter question. I would suggest that neither matter is at all clear, and it may be instructive to remember that 1 Clement has to deal with a revolt against the *presbyteroi*. Given that the proper order of the household based on proper respect for its various officers is the basic subject of these letters, could it not be that those who

---

[14] The first is Deut. 25.4, used by Paul in 1 Cor. 9.9 to confirm that a workman has a right to share in the harvest, though Paul forgoes his claim. It is here quoted in a slightly different text form, and neither NT form of the quotation exactly corresponds to the LXX. The second is not found in the Jewish scriptures, but appears in the Mission Discourse of Matthew/Luke (Matt. 10.10; Luke 10.7). Presumably both were transmitted orally in the church and classically used to justify apostles' pay.

[15] See citations in n. 11 above.

[16] George W. Knight III reviews the discussion, pp. 236–7. Cf. Kelly, pp. 126–7; Hanson, pp. 102–3.

persist in sin are precisely those who challenge or refuse to accept the teaching of those 'seniors' who bear the tradition and have been put in a particular paid position in the community precisely for the purpose of preserving that tradition?

Such a reading would suggest something like the following scenario: as in any household of antiquity, age bore with it a certain status and authority. It was the older people who were guardians of the corporate memory. They were not to be lightly disregarded, still less corrected. Timothy himself was to deal with his elders respectfully. Among the older members of the community certain people had emerged who did a particularly good job as the bearers of that memory and the teachers of the tradition, and these received an honorarium for their valuable contribution. The evidence of Papias confirms both the survival of the term *presbyteros* in its usual sense of a 'senior person', and its association with the apostolic tradition.[17]

So far, then, we do not appear to be dealing with an office comparable to that of the *episkopos*. Certainly in 1 Timothy it would appear that the only constituted officers of the local church, if they can be appropriately described thus, are the 'head-stewards' (*episkopoi*) and 'servants' (*diakonoi*) (as indeed we find already in Phil. 1.1); these and these only are dealt with in what seems like an ordered code. The *presbyteroi* would seem to come into a different kind of category. But that is to

---

[17] 'I shall not hesitate to furnish you, along with the interpretations, with all that in days gone by I carefully learnt from the presbyters* and have carefully recalled, for I can guarantee its truth ... And whenever anyone came who had been a follower of the presbyters,** I enquired into the words of the presbyters,** what Andrew or Peter had said, or Philip or Thomas or James or John or Matthew, or any other disciple of the Lord, and what Aristion and the presbyter John, disciples of the Lord, were still saying' (as quoted by Eusebius, *Historia Ecclesiastica* III.39, ET G. A. Williamson, Penguin Classics (Harmondsworth, 1965)). On the two occasions I have marked 'presbyter' with a double asterisk, the term seems to refer to the Apostles. Aristion and the 'presbyter John' seem to belong to the next generation, but given the usage for Apostles, it is hazardous to treat 'presbyter' as a term of office in these cases. The first use, marked with one asterisk, seems to be a general reference to people Papias could consult, older people who had access to authentic oral tradition. If nothing else, this second-century statement indicates a confusion of terminology. Leaping to the conclusion that a clearly defined presbyteral office already exists is likely to be hazardous.

ignore two tantalising hints, the suggestion that some *presbyteroi* preside in 1 Tim. 5.17 and the appearance of the term *presbyterion*, or 'presbyterate' in 1 Tim. 4.14, referring apparently to the authoritative body which laid hands on 'Timothy'. It seems we have to reckon with the presbyterate being a more formal body than simply the senior members of the community (though the 'ordination' of Timothy is not consistently depicted: in 2 Tim. 1.6, Paul seems to have laid on hands, whereas in 1 Tim. 4.14 it is the presbyterate).

It is difficult, then, to deduce the relationship of *episkopos* and *presbyteroi* from texts which are not explicitly concerned with that issue, and never overtly address the question. Can the issue be resolved in another way? I suggest it may. In recent sociological studies, the household analogy has been dominant. Perhaps this has overshadowed another crucial parallel which certainly had an influence on the early Christians, namely the Jewish community and their synagogue organisation. The hypothesis, admittedly tentative, is that the Pastorals reflect a stage in which there is a perceptible shift in the principal way Christians were identifying themselves socially – from 'God's household' to 'God's people'.

This was hardly a radical new departure. Whether or not Paul in some sense self-consciously exchanged being a rabbi in a synagogue for being a 'sophist' in Judge's sense, he carried with him a set of Jewish assumptions and practices which explain that unusual feature in the work of a popular philosopher, 'the establishment of a set of corporate societies'. Paul tended to expect these societies to function rather roughly on the lines of the Jewish community (e.g. constituting a court rather than going to civil courts, as in 1 Cor. 6.1ff.), an expectation that his converts in Corinth seem not to have understood fully. But as time went on, I suggest, there was a tendency for formalisation according to established Jewish patterns and structures, and the organisation implied in the Pastorals reflects increasing influence from Jewish precedent.

By the time of Philippians, the gifts of administration that Paul had mentioned among the charismatic endowments of the Body of Christ (1 Cor. 12.27ff.) had become invested in *episko-*

poi and *diakonoi* (Phil. 1.1). Their titles reflect their 'household' functions. They ordered the life of the community, which literally met in a 'house' and metaphorically functioned as 'God's household', sharing a meal together. They appear in the greeting of that letter naturally and without comment, their existence and role part of the shared assumptions between author and readers. There is no sign of any *presbyteroi* in the authentic Pauline material: they are a feature of Acts and the Pastorals.

But *presbyteroi* appear in the gospels because there were Jewish 'elders', sometimes described as 'the elders of the people'. Since the time of Antiochus Epiphanes, Jerusalem had been governed, like other cities with Greek constitutions, by a *Gerousia*,[18] a term which implies that the membership of the council would be the elderly, experienced and wise senior citizens. The councillors are referred to as *presbyteroi* in Josephus from the first century, and the term is used in the gospels for those who led the community, with the Sadducees and Pharisees, in the Sanhedrin (*synedrion* is another Greek term, which appeared in Hebrew as a loan-word, and refers to the same council).[19]

Jewish *presbyteroi*, then, appear to be community leaders, and although local conditions seem to have varied a good deal, this is largely confirmed for other Jewish communities in both Palestine and the Diaspora. The civic authority which governed a Jewish community in a Greek city, with certain constitutional powers granted in relation to their own ethnic community, would be a council of *archontes*, 'rulers', or *presbyteroi*.[20]

These 'elders' were not synagogue officials. Where larger

[18] For the information offered here, see the new Schürer, *The History of the Jewish People*, vol. II, pp. 203–4, 423–63; and vol. III, revised and edited by Geza Vermes, Fergus Millar and Martin Goodman (Edinburgh, 1986), pp. 87–107. Also see *The Jewish People in the First Century*, vol. I, ed. S. Safrai and M. Stern with D. Flusser and W. C. van Unnik (Assen, 1974), chapter 7.

[19] See E. P. Sanders, *Judaism: Practice and Belief 63 BCE–66 CE* (London, 1992), pp. 472ff. on the Sanhedrin.

[20] *Presbyteroi* was certainly used for this council in Palestine, less certainly in the Diaspora. But see Safrai and Stern, *The Jewish People*, chapter 8.

Jewish communities existed, there would be more than one
synagogue, and archaeological and other evidence suggests
that like Christian churches, synagogues (or assemblies) were
often held in household settings. The council of elders probably
had among its responsibilities the appointment of synagogue
officials. Reading the prayers, reading scripture and preaching
were not duties specific to particular officers, but someone had
to arrange for members of the congregation to fulfil those
functions, and provide for the orderly prosecution of the
congregation's Sabbath duties. The responsible administrator
of the synagogue was the *rōsh ha-knesset*, or *archisynagōgos*;[21]
other officers included the person responsible for the alms
contributed by the congregation, and the 'servant' (*chazan
ha-knesset, diakonos* or *hypēretēs*) who performed those practical
offices such as fetching the rolls of scripture from the ark,
blowing the trumpet, etc. That *presbyteroi* and synagogue
officials like the *archisynagogoi*, etc. had distinct functions seems
clear.

Too great confidence is precluded by the state of the evidence and a certain fluidity of terminology. But this situation is
highly suggestive in relation to our material. Called an *episkopos*
by long-standing Christian habit, the administrator began to
acquire the functions of the *archisynagogos*, and the existing
diakonoi fulfilled in the Christian community the tasks of the
synagogue almoner and the synagogue attendant. Meanwhile,
Christians, being excluded like Jews by their religious scruples
from many normal civic functions, began to organise themselves as a kind of distinct 'ethnic' community, later to be
known as the 'third race', neither Jew nor Gentile, and confess-
ing to 'heavenly' citizenship. Their 'seniors' began not only to
have the honour that came from age and the respect that came
from being those who held the corporate memory, but also to
be constituted into a governing council, which had the authority to appoint and advise the *episkopos*. The fact that Timothy

---

[21] The curious references to women and children holding the title are later and
apparently honorific. The problems of the evidence are discussed in the new
Schürer, vol. III.1, pp. 101ff. Paul Trebilco, *Jewish Communities in Asia Minor*, SNTS
Monograph Series 69 (Cambridge, 1991), argues otherwise.

and Titus, the apostolic delegates, are depicted in the Pastorals as appointing them links this with their function of preserving the apostolic tradition.

Such a picture accords with other evidence,[22] such as the *Didascalia*, where, as in the Pastorals, there is no specific section on the *presbyteroi*. They appear, however, as receiving hospitality and bounties like the widows, but double since they are 'honoured as the apostles and counsellors of the bishop', and as 'the crown of the church' as its 'moderators and councillors'. Ignatius also speaks of the *presbyteroi* as 'God's *synedrion*' and the 'council' (*synedrion*) or 'college (*syndesmos*) of the apostles'.[23] The *presbyteroi* therefore constitute a church council, and are the guardians of the apostolic tradition.

In this way, a plausible picture can be reached of how the *episkopos* was related to the *presbyteroi*, and one that fits the ambiguous evidence of the Pastorals, which presumably date in any case from a transitional period. The theological outlook implied by a community having such a 'council' coheres with the claims both to universalism and to particular election we have observed earlier. It suggests an implicit assumption that the church supersedes the Jewish people as God's chosen race, a claim which grew and developed through the second century.

THE 'DIAKONOI'

So we turn to the other administrative office, and it should be clear by now that the argument of this section will encourage both an almost literal understanding of the term *diakonos* as 'servant' within the metaphor of God's household, and a respect for the 'attendant' who acts as functionary, as the parallel figure in the synagogue did, for the church assembly for worship and teaching. The two 'models' come together, given that, as well as teaching, these communities presumably

---

[22] The arguments have been presented in a note 'On *Episkopos* and *Presbyteros*', to be published in the *Journal of Theological Studies* in 1993.
[23] See citations in n. 11 above.

shared a real or symbolic eucharistic meal, at which the *diako-noi* would serve.

The directions in the Pastorals concerning these officers, like the others, are concerned not with functions, but moral quali-ties, indeed very much the same qualities as those enjoined upon the *episkopos* and *presbyteroi*. The *diakonoi* are to be *semnoi*, worthy of respect, not given to double-talk, not partial to much wine, not grasping in a dishonest way, holding the mystery of the faith with a pure conscience (1 Tim. 3.8–9). They are to be tested and proved before appointment, and then being *anenkle-toi*, irreproachable, they may perform their service (3.10). They are to be husbands of one wife, and good at managing their children and their own households (3.12).

We have heard such injunctions before – the same high standards are expected of *diakonoi* as of *presbyteroi* or *episkopos*. We are further told that *diakonoi* who perform their office well create a good position for themselves and have much *parrhēsia*, that boldness and freedom of speech which the Cynic philoso-phers claimed, in the faith which is in Christ Jesus (3.13). They too, it seems, are involved in the guidance and reproof of the community, as well as the 'serving' functions we presuppose, and they clearly have standing and authority in the life of the community. They are no 'mere servants'!

Paul had used the term *diakonos* of himself, as he had used also the term *doulos*, slave: he was slave of Jesus Christ and servant of the new covenant, the ambassador who brought God's message of peace on God's behalf.[24] In the Pastorals, Timothy is to be *diakonos* of Jesus Christ (1 Tim. 4.6) and *doulos* of the Lord (2 Tim. 2.24); clearly in neither case is the term used in any kind of technical sense, but rather it carries with it the notion that the 'man of God' (a term used in 1 Tim. 6.11 and 2 Tim. 3.17) is God's agent, and acts with God's authority, like the managerial slaves described in the previous chapter. Presumably, however, as in any household or business operation, there were slaves and slaves, servants and servants,

---

[24] Paul as *doulos:* Rom. 1.1; Gal. 1.10; Phil. 1.1; and copied in Titus 1.1. Paul as *diakonos* of new covenant: 2 Cor. 3, cf. 2 Cor. 5.18–20; as *diakonos* of the gospel: Eph. 3.7; Col. 1.23.

different grades and ranks, though the same high moral standards, and the same commitment and loyalty to the master, were expected of all.

The new issue here, however, concerns the roles permitted to women in the 'household of God'. Tucked in the middle of the only passage to deal with *diakonoi* (1 Tim. 3.8–13) is an intriguing sentence: 'The women likewise are to be *semnai*, worthy of respect, not *diaboloi*, slanderers [hardly 'devils' here!], *nephalioi*, temperate with wine, and faithful [or loyal] in everything' (3.11). In other words, these women too are to have the qualities of other church functionaries; but then they are presumably qualities expected of the whole church membership, with the officers setting an example. The question is whether the word translated 'women', *gynaikes*, should be taken in the sense 'wives', meaning the wives of the *diakonoi*, or in the sense 'women who are *diakonoi*' in their own right.

The latter seems to be the more plausible reading. That women did function as *diakonoi* is clear from the case of Phoebe (Rom. 16.1). The sentence shape is exactly parallel to that which introduced the *diakonoi* (verse 8) as next in the list to be considered. That said, however, the female servants in a household probably did not have identical functions to those of male servants, and the argument of this chapter is that the 'literal' meaning of these 'metaphorical' official terms is still much alive. Women may have been allowed to serve at table from the early days of the church, but 1 Corinthians suggests that there were reservations about women 'teaching' even in days when they may have 'prophesied'.

There is no question but that such reservations are sharply in evidence in these letters. Women at the church assemblies are to learn in silence and submission. The author does not permit a woman to teach or have authority over a man (perhaps meaning her husband) (1 Tim. 2.9–12). Scriptural warrant is given for this ruling. The statements are so strong that one must probably deduce that there were women attempting to exercise leadership, and many scholars have suggested that the Pastorals represent a situation in which the freedom and charisma of the earliest churches is being suppressed by progressive patriarchalisation. The biblically based argument establishing the hierarchy of husband and wife on the basis of Adam's priority and Eve's fault would seem to support this judgment.

The element which has perhaps been understressed is the influence of Jewish practice. The synagogue quorum requires men, and men have the obligation of praying and fulfilling the required religious duties; women who attend synagogue sit apart. Women are freed from such public religious obligations, but have others in the ritual of the home. In other words, roles are sharply differentiated. The likelihood is that these customs were already usual at this time, though evidence for a separate women's gallery in synagogues is later than this period. Such an assumption, however, both explains Paul's response in 1 Corinthians and the hardening line found in the Pastoral epistles.

For Christians, however, ambiguity would continue. For in certain respects the church saw itself as God's family, and on the domestic scene, in the family, the wife of the household head had both status and religious obligations. Christian gatherings included eating together in God's household, and women had, it seemed, acted as *diakonoi* in that context, presumably waiting at table. Furthermore, the church would continue to appoint women as *diakonoi* to attend as maid-servants at the baptism of women, for decency's sake. There was a certain tension between the two 'models' which informed the church's self-understanding as a community.

And probably there were other factors which explain the stance of the letters in relation to women, as we saw in the opening chapter. These become the more crucial as we try to assess the duties and roles of widows in these early Christian communities.

THE WIDOWS

Earlier discussions have highlighted the principal difficulty of reaching conclusions about formal or institutionalised offices in the church(es) to which these letters refer, namely that the 'duty-codes' seem to be an adaptation of household codes in the direction of a church order or canon, and some part of the letters retain the old household 'duty-code' elements. We have already met this problem in relation to the *presbyteroi*; it emerges again with the widows. Are widows appointed to some kind of 'order' or clerical rank? Or are they just dependent unfortunates?

The answer is probably neither. We are a long way, I suggest, from the formally developed clerical and monastic orders of later ecclesiastical organisation, and we have to be careful not to use language which by implication projects back a later situation. We must be all the more careful not to queer the historical picture by a desire to justify women's ministry or ordination in the modern context.[25]

Let us examine carefully what is found in the text of these letters. The passage dealing with widows (1 Tim. 5.3ff.) opens by ordering that 'honour' be given to the 'real widows' (*tas ontōs chēras*). Who are these 'real widows'? Some have argued that the phrase refers to those who belong to a constituted order of enrolled widows, but the context does not seem to support this.

The passage proceeds to indicate that if a widow has children or grandchildren, they should be responsible for her upkeep, showing their 'piety' towards their own 'house' and repaying their debt to their parents. The 'real widow', it goes on, one who is alone in the world, hopes in God. Later (verse 8) the point is stressed again that anyone who does not make provision for his relations has denied the faith and is worse than an unbeliever. This seems to imply that the 'real widow' is the one genuinely bereft of normal means of support, and that the church is already undertaking to support by charitable offerings those in this situation.

The background to all this is the fact that a woman was legally, and usually financially, dependent on first her father,

---

[25] Neither of these dangers is avoided by Bonnie Bowman Thurston in *The Widows: A Women's Ministry in the Early Church* (Minneapolis, 1989). Nevertheless, the book provides a survey of the relevant material both within and beyond the New Testament.

then her husband,[26] coupled with the practical reality that
life-expectancy was far less in pre-modern conditions than we
usually take for granted, so that it was far from unlikely that a
woman would be left destitute, even at an early age, unless the
husband's heirs took responsibility for her. Jewish practice was
to give alms for widows and orphans, and this is described in
James 1.27 as the first feature of pure and faultless religion.
There is plenty of evidence[27] that, as well as continuing Jewish
precedent, Christians took responsibility for their widowed
members as the 'household of God'. Now some seem to have
taken to presuming that the church would care for widowed
members, and they need not fulfil their filial obligations.

The 'real widow' must surely be the one who requires help.
What has clouded the discussion is that this 'real widow' not
only hopes in God, but remains in prayer day and night. From
this it has been deduced that she has certain spiritual duties.
But ancient society was built upon conventions of 'give and
take', reciprocal duties.[28] In return for patronage, a client
would lend support and further the reputation of the one to
whom he owed an obligation of thanks. Centuries later, with
similar presuppositions about mutual social obligations, John
Chrysostom would make it quite clear that the rich had an
obligation to help the poor, and in return the poor had an
obligation to pray for the rich.[29] What these epistles seem to be
facing is a situation in which some widows are accepting
charitable help from the church either unjustifiably, or in the
wrong spirit. If a widow takes advantage of the church's
almsgiving to live self-indulgently, then she is as good as dead
(verse 6). A 'proper widow' is one who both needs assistance

[26] Ben Witherington III, *Women in the Earliest Churches*; Averil Cameron and Amélie
Kuhrt, *Images of Women in Late Antiquity* (Detroit, 1983).

[27] Apart from the Pastorals and Jas 1.27, within the NT the classic evidence is Acts
6.1; 9.39, 41. For the extra-canonical evidence, see article in *Encyclopedia of Early
Christianity*, ed. Everett Ferguson, Michael McHugh and Frederick W. Norris (New
York and London, 1990); and Thurston, *The Widows*.

[28] See above, pp. 18 and 34.

[29] See my 'Christian Attitides to Finance in the First Four Centuries', *Epworth Review* 4
(1977), 78–86.

and receives it responsibly, setting an example of faith and piety.

The charge to honour the 'real widows' does not imply more than that. It need mean no more than that you should respect them as you would your grandmother, a sentiment that used to be much more common than it has become in our society. Such a reading is encouraged by the context: in the previous verse, Timothy has been told to advise or encourage older women as mothers.

But the questions are not yet all resolved. For in verse 9 we read: 'Let a woman be enrolled as a widow if she is not less than sixty years old, the wife of one husband, and publicly known for good works, if she has borne children, given hospitality to strangers, washed the feet of the saints, supported those who are oppressed, and taken every opportunity to do good.' Who are these 'enrolled widows'? Do they constitute an 'order'?

Not, I think, in the sense some have hoped for. The roll, it would seem, is the list of those who are to receive alms and charitable assistance. Only the elderly should qualify. Younger widows are to be refused (verse 11). Reasons are given: they get distracted from Christ and want to get married after all, and so attract the charge of abandoning their first commitment (verses 11–12). Besides this, they learn to be idle and go around visiting households, not only practising idleness but becoming gossips and busy-bodies, speaking of things better left unsaid. So these younger widows should remarry, bear children, manage a household, and provide no opportunity to the enemy for slander (verses 13–14). Now, some scholars have deduced from this description that widows enrolled in the 'order' not only had duties of prayer and intercession, but functions such as house-to-house visiting.[30] These were being improperly performed by the younger widows. I would suggest, however, that the explanation of these verses is quite different.

The issues centre on the celibate lifestyle. That devotion to

---

[30] E.g. Thurston, *The Widows*. Kelly, Hanson and other commentators assume an 'order' of widows with religious duties expected in return for support.

Christ could be expressed by a radical rejection of the normal social values is evident, as we have seen, from much early Christian literature. The Pastorals themselves honour those who have been married only once, yet there is much evidence from the ancient world of women being widowed well before the age of thirty. It is conceivable that many in that position were attracted, as the legendary Thecla had been, to an ideology of continence. Indeed, in an important study of sexual renunciation in early Christianity, Peter Brown has argued that most of the 'virgins' were ex-married men and women, in fact, those widowed.[31]

A number of factors encouraged such a radical lifestyle. One was Paul's own teaching: 'Blessed are they who have kept the flesh pure, for they shall become a Temple of God', we found in the Acts of Paul and Thecla;[32] 'Do you not know that your body is a temple of the indwelling Holy Spirit?' wrote Paul, 'and the Spirit of God is God's gift to you' (1 Cor. 6.19). True, Paul was struggling with sexual sins (*porneia*) rather than enjoining celibacy, but his insistence on honouring God in the body could easily be taken more radically than he intended, especially in the light of his tortuous argument in 1 Corinthians 7. Another was the association of abstention from sex with prophecy: 'Blessed are the continent, for to them God will speak' is another telling saying in the Acts of Paul and Thecla.[33] Certainly in the Syrian Orient we find forms of Christianity which demanded celibacy of every baptised believer;[34] the roots of such practice in the second century seem to lie deep. It was not just gnosticism or apocalypticism that fostered an ascetic lifestyle, but the radical form of Christian-

---

[31] Peter Brown, *The Body and Society: Men, Women and Sexual Renunciation in Early Christianity* (London, 1989).

[32] See above, p. 14.

[33] The same context as the words noted earlier (see p. 14 above): Acts of Paul and Thecla 4, ET Hennecke and Schneemelcher, *New Testament Apocrypha*, vol. II, p. 354.

[34] A. Vööbus, *A History of Asceticism in the Syrian Orient*, CSCO 184 (Louvain, 1958). See also Brown, *The Body and Society*. The Encratites appear in the catalogues of heresies drawn up by the church Fathers (e.g. Irenaeus, Hippolytus, Epiphanius) and are associated with Tatian, the pupil of Justin Martyr who composed the *Diatessaron* (the first harmony of the four gospels) and evangelised Syria.

ity known as encratism. Perhaps it is not for nothing that the Pastorals ask *enkrateia*, continence, of their church leaders.

These verses about the young widows seem to presuppose that they have made a vow or commitment to be espoused to Christ. This is not to be despised. What is disapproved is the tendency for younger widows to bring the whole thing into disrepute by failing to live up to it. They are distracted by a good offer of marriage, and their piety is thrown over. Celibacy brings its own dangers, and as Paul had suggested, marriage is a good curb on the passions of the young (1 Cor. 7.9).

But the other problem is the unemployment of free young women with no household of which to be mistress. Whether just gossip is at issue is a matter that cannot be settled from these verses, but reading between the lines one can hear the same suspicion of irregular teaching by unauthorised persons as other early Christian texts display in relation to the spread of gnostic ideas. D. R. MacDonald notes that it was widely believed in the ancient world that women were particularly prone to be led astray, and since they largely lacked formal education, it is perhaps not surprising that they had no criteria or framework for making sensible judgments. Women were also commonly associated with the telling of tales – indeed, Plato thinks it necessary to control the stories told to children by women. So, MacDonald suggests, the legends found in the Acts of Paul are likely to have been passed on in women's circles: hence the warning against 'old wives' tales' in 1 Tim. 4.7.[35] In ancient texts it is not unknown for husbands to be told to teach their young wives philosophy,[36] and a young widow was deprived of that guidance. The false teachers are described in 2 Tim. 3.6ff. as the sort who insinuate themselves into houses and get silly women into their clutches. These women are

[35] MacDonald, *The Legend and the Apostle*. This study is illuminating. The argument is that the stories collected in The Acts of Paul were oral narratives told by 'celibate women in Asia Minor who expected Christ soon to destroy the world and to rescue the righteous. This apocalypticism was attended by contempt for Asia Minor social institutions, especially the household' (p. 37). Tertullian apparently knew some people who told the story of Thecla to legitimate women teaching and baptising.

[36] E.g. Plutarch, *Advice to the Bride and Groom* 144D–F, referred to by Verner, *The Household of God*, p. 68. See discussion above, pp. 82–3.

described as anxious to learn, but incapable of reaching knowledge of the truth. The 'things better left unspoken' could very well be precisely the teaching(s) of which these letters disapprove, teaching which may itself have encouraged the rejection of normal societal relations for a radical asceticism.

It is noticeable that the teaching which the older women are supposed to offer to younger women in Titus 2.3–5 is the precise counterbalance to any idealisation of celibacy: they are to set an example by not scandal-mongering, but being reverent in demeanour, and teaching the younger women to be loving wives and mothers, temperate, chaste, busy at home, kind and respecting the authority of their husbands.

There seems little ground, then, for seeing here any evidence of an order engaged in house-to-house pastoral visiting, or any other formalised church ministry. The final statement in this section tends to confirm this conclusion. A Christian woman with widows in the family is enjoined not to expect the church to care for her widowed relatives. Presumably this statement refers to upper-class wealthy women, the sort who headed households and had a certain financial independence; Christian women in this position often appear as patrons of local churches or of particular Christian teachers,[37] and maybe they thought supporting the church was a way of providing for their own dependants. The reason given for this injunction is that the church should be free to support those who really are widows – and surely this must mean those who have no means of support.

It is worth noting also that the whole section occurs, not in the place where the character of the church officials is discussed, but in the section beginning with the older and younger men and women, and ending with slaves. True, the paid presbyters appear here too, but if the argument of an earlier section holds, they are not so much 'officers' as the respected wise men of the community, who, like the real widows, receive a 'pension' from the church, and in return set an example and perform good works.

[37] E.g. possibly Lydia in Acts 16; probably Chloe in 1 Cor. 1.11. Judge (in the article 'The Early Christians as a Scholastic Community') identifies fifteen patrons, six of them women.

CONCLUSION

Although it is not explicitly stated, the Pastorals do seem to take seriously the call and responsibility of every Christian to be loyal and to behave in ways that will not bring the church into disrepute. This may be deduced from what is expected of slaves. Every Christian belongs to God's household, every Christian receives the grace and salvation of God. But serious questions have arisen concerning what the implications are for living in the world, and how the will of God is mediated. The answer of the Pastorals is that, as in the social institutions then familiar, the hierarchy of servants passes down the orders of the one who is ruler or head of the community, both by precept and by example.

It is particularly important, therefore, that those who have leadership roles in the church set a good example of correct ethical behaviour. This is spelt out in terms of key qualities, but also in terms of proper relationships between the various ranks within God's household. Contemporary society conferred both authority and indeed obligation on the various ranks of the hierarchy, and the Pastorals never question those assumptions.

What we have here is not a church canon establishing clerical orders whose functions are clearly delineated. To suppose that is to project back what developed later. Here the ministry of the church is still only in embryo, but the stress on authoritative teaching, and on proper hierarchical relationships modelled on a typical Greco-Roman household, laid the foundations for the development that would gather pace through the second century. The rather everyday terms used of servants in a household and seniors in a community achieve technical usage, three clerical orders emerge, and women become progressively marginalised within the system.

Here, the 'servants' and 'slaves' in God's household are the stewards of God's mysteries, with God's authority vested in them. They are also stewards of a tradition that has reached them through Paul. Paul is the guarantor, and the real authority behind these texts. It is to the portrait of Paul, and the transmission of the Pauline tradition through these texts, that we must turn next.

CHAPTER 6

The contribution of the Pastorals to the reception of Paul as an Apostle

One of the problems of the Pastorals in modern times has been the rather stale, defensive debate about Pauline authorship. After what has been said so far, it is possible to see how the ground can be shifted, and a more positive approach developed. Modern assumptions focus on individuals, but Paul, remarkable man though he must have been, was deeply incorporated into a community. Waiving the question of authenticity for the moment, the Pauline letters are almost invariably co-authored: 1 Corinthians is sent from Paul and Sosthenes, 2 Corinthians, Philippians and Colossians from Paul and Timothy, 1 and 2 Thessalonians from Paul, Silvanus and Timothy; even that most personal letter to the Galatians associates 'all the brethren with me' in Paul's opening greetings. So Romans and Ephesians are the exceptions that prove the rule. Paul worked with associates and assistants, through fellow-travellers and networks of communication, and relied on local leadership – he only wrote letters when things broke down.

But clearly the network of followers and communities which he thus formed had a special, if sometimes troubled, relationship with him, and despite his attempts to encourage mature independence, sometimes these Gentiles diverged so unexpectedly and so far from his Jewish presumptions that he found himself attempting to assert authority over them. For the sake of order and decency, Paul himself had encouraged converts to maintain the social *status quo*, giving far from radical advice on the place of women and slaves. Already in his lifetime, assuming the authenticity of Philippians, local leadership offices were being established, modelled on household service and administration, and probably carrying considerable authority.

The Pastorals reveal to us the development that took place in the Pauline communities as they were distanced from Paul. Naturally enough, his image has been enhanced and domesticated, and he has become the model, example and authority to which people look up, and from which the tradition is believed to have received both its authorisation and the guarantee of its validity. So the portrait of Paul presented in these letters is integral to their argument.

To explore what kind of figure Paul has become, it is necessary to begin by looking closely at the content of these texts. Then the implication of his being presented as their author must be considered.

SOME KEY PASSAGES

1 Timothy 1.12–16

Paul is portrayed as giving thanks to the one who has empowered him, Christ Jesus our Lord. Though using an un-Pauline verb, *endunamoō*, this properly represents Paul's understanding of his own apostleship as presented in 2 Corinthians: his sufficiency for the task of being *diakonos* of the new covenant is not of himself, but of God (2 Cor. 3.5), and thanksgiving to the God who carries him around as captive in his triumphal procession was expressed just a few verses earlier (2 Cor. 2.14). A little later Paul will acknowledge that he has this ministry through having received mercy (2 Cor. 4.1). Here in the Pastorals, thanks are offered for thinking Paul trustworthy enough for service when he was formerly a blasphemer, persecutor and insulter. He was treated with mercy, however (1 Tim. 1.13), because he did it unknowingly as an unbeliever. At this point, anyone deeply read in the Pauline material becomes a little uneasy: Paul would surely not have made such an excuse, conscious though he was of God's mercy in calling him to his service (Gal. 1.13–15; 2 Cor. 4.1), and of his former position as a persecutor (Gal. 1.13–14; Phil. 3.5–6).

The grace of our Lord, however, was abundant with the faith and love which is in Christ Jesus. This statement is supported by a 'faithful saying': Christ Jesus came into the world to save sinners. Paul is then presented as the supreme model of the saved sinner, 'of whom I am the first', even though Paul himself had claimed to be 'blameless according to the Law' in Philippians – not a 'Gentile sinner'. Here, however, he appears as having received mercy so that Christ Jesus might display all his patience in him first, as a 'type' of those who would come to believe in him for eternal life. Now we understand why he has appeared as a sinner excusing himself for unknowingly persecuting and harrying Christians before his conversion: Paul has become the prototype convert, typical of those who were to be found in the Pauline churches.

2 Timothy 1.11 ff.

Having spoken of salvation in Christ, 'Paul' continues, 'Of this gospel I have been appointed herald, apostle, and teacher.' Paul's claim to be an Apostle was contested in Corinth and is certainly based in his own self-understanding, but he never called himself a *keryx*, despite speaking of the *kerygma* and even 'my *kerygma*', nor did he use the term *didaskalos* of himself. His role as the ambassador who delivered the new covenant and founded church communities has here been redescribed, with particular emphases which make him the fountainhead of the tradition, and of the teaching which is so important in these letters.

This is confirmed by what follows. The passage goes on first to explain that this is the reason for Paul's present plight, presumably an allusion to his being in prison, which will soon appear explicitly as the context of this writing, then to assert that he is not ashamed of his situation, and so to provide the reason why. The reason is that he knows in whom he has placed his trust, no doubt implying God, and he is persuaded that he (God) is able to guard 'my deposit' or perhaps 'what has been entrusted to me' until that day. The word is *parathēkē*, the noun from the root which means 'to pass on as a tradition'.

It is by no means clear whether it means what Paul had passed to him, or what he passed on, but does it really matter? The point is the tradition that has come through him to the reader of these letters. The next sentence is a command: the reader (Timothy, or indeed any church teacher) is to hold to the 'type' of the healthy words heard from Paul, and 'to guard the good deposit through the Holy Spirit dwelling in us'.

Now, however, the issue concerning the shame of being imprisoned is taken up more fully. Paul has been abandoned by everybody in the province of Asia (verse 15), including Phrygelus and Hermogenes. Onesiphorus, however, has often brought him relief. He was not ashamed to visit a prisoner. He is given much commendation. As we move into chapter 2, the reader is told to take strength (the word is *endunamoō*, again, recalling the description of God as the one who empowered Paul) from the grace which is in Christ Jesus. He is to take his share of hardship, like a good soldier. Paul was not only the one who taught this (as we have meanwhile been reminded again explicitly in 2.2, where the passing on of his teaching is also again emphasised), but one who embodied it. And those who turned away from him or supported him are likewise exemplary. As argued in chapter 2, the Pauline communities envisaged in these letters are insecure in the world, and need empowering for facing public disgrace, though carefully taught not to seek notoriety for the wrong reasons. Paul becomes the model of the martyr, his associates models of appropriate response to those who suffer for the faith.

The theme continues as 'Paul' urges the reader to reflect on all this, assuring him or her that the Lord will give understanding. A reminder is given of Jesus Christ risen from the dead, 'according to my Gospel'. For that gospel, Paul suffers chains like a criminal, but the Word of God is not bound in fetters. So Paul endures everything for the elect, for the sake of their salvation. The point is pressed home with a 'faithful saying' concerning dying and rising with Christ, enduring and reigning with him, and the consequences of denying him.

The thrust of 2 Timothy, then, is to create a model of the martyr living out the Pauline gospel grounded in the death and resurrection of Christ. Paul himself becomes the exemplification of this witness.

2 Timothy 3.10–12

These verses confirm that general estimate. After a series of exhortations, Paul reappears as example: 'You, my son, have attended closely to my teaching and manner of life, my resolution, faith, patience, love, endurance, the persecutions and sufferings – all I went through in Antioch, Iconium, Lystra, the persecutions I endured and from them all the Lord saved me.' The specific references to Paul's life, and the repetition of his own phraseology (compare the last clause with 2 Cor. 1.10), are then applied in a generalisation: all who want to live with piety (the un-Pauline, *eusebōs*) in Christ Jesus will be persecuted.

2 Timothy 4.6–8

Paul is depicted as saying that he is already poured out like a libation, and the occasion of his dissolution is upon him. In Philippians, similar usage is found where Paul speaks of his imminent death; there the libation is poured out on the sacrifice of their faith. The metaphor is then changed: 'I have run the great race; I have completed the run; I have kept the faith. And now there awaits me the garland of righteousness which the Lord, the righteous judge, will award me on that day.' The first phrase uses the same language as 1 Tim. 6.12, in both cases the meaning being 'contest', and like 2 Tim. 2.5 envisaging an athletics match of some kind, often wrestling but perhaps here specified by the succeeding phrase, which speaks of completing the 'run'. The prize at the games was always the garland of olive, worn with pride. So much is clear, but for our purposes it is important to note again that Paul's sacrifice and his confident expectation of winning are by implication exemplary. The prize is 'not for me alone, but for all who have set their hearts on his epiphany'.

2 Timothy 4.9–end

This passage rehearses a series of personal details, messages, and greetings. Paul appears as having everyday needs, friends and enemies. The significance of this will be discussed later, but it is mentioned here as contributing to the picture of Paul that is built up in these letters. For once there is no exemplary motive explicit. But implicitly there may be. Paul is presented as alone and needing support, as we gather from earlier in the letter, because he is in prison. He was let down in court since none of his supporters turned up. He had support from the Lord, and was rescued for the sake of proclaiming the gospel. That such an account of his position was intended to encourage or rebuke the reader(s) is far from implausible in the light of the rest of this letter.

Titus 3.3–8

Most of this letter is a summary of the main points of teaching to be passed on, but in these verses 'we' become a model. This time it is again a model of conversion, as in the example from 1 Timothy above. 'Paul' identifies with other Christians. There was a time when 'we' were foolish, disobedient (or perhaps, unbelieving), in error, slaves to all sorts of desires and pleasures, living in wickedness and envy, hated and hating one another. There follows a statement of the saving gospel which we examined in chapter 3. Previously in 2.12, we have read that 'we' are disciplined by God's grace to renounce godless ways and worldly desires, and to live a life of temperance, righteousness and godliness in the present age. The problem is that Paul would certainly not have identified himself as a slave to desires and pleasures, living in wickedness, or needing that kind of disciplining, as we noted before. What is quite clear, however, is that he has become an example for the preaching of the gospel.

Thus the whole tone of the descriptions of Paul in these epistles suggests that he is intended to appear as an unquestioned authority, the ideal missionary and Apostle, example to all, the model or paradigm convert, the Christian leader to be imitated. Such a conclusion marries well with the picture of the theology of these epistles developed previously in this study. Paul is the authoritative teacher by precept and example, whose tradition is continued by his successors, and their appointees.

SOME COMPARISONS

It is in the Apocryphal Acts and similar material that we find the most suggestive parallels to this.

In the Acts of Peter, there is a description of Peter's first preaching in Rome.[1] It is set on the first day of the week, and a multitude is assembled. Peter proceeds to have a speech attributed to him, not unlike the way speeches appear in the canonical Acts.

You men who are present here, who hope in Christ, you who have suffered temptation for a little, attend! ... Because [mankind] through ignorance fell into death in their many and varied weaknesses, almighty God, moved with compassion, sent his Son into the world; and I was with him. And I walked on the water, and myself survive as a witness of it; I confess that I was there when formerly in the world he was at work with the signs and all the miracles which he performed. Dearest brethren, I denied our Lord Jesus Christ, and not once only, but three times. For there were wicked dogs who came about me, as said the prophet of the Lord. But the Lord did not lay it to my charge; he turned to me and had compassion on the weakness of my flesh, so that afterwards I wept bitterly and lamented the weakness of my faith, because I was made senseless by the devil and did not keep my Lord's words in mind. And now I tell you, men and brethren, who have come together in the name of Jesus Christ: Satan the deceiver points his arrows at you too, that you may depart from the way. But do not be disloyal, brethren, nor let your spirit fall, but be strong and stand fast and do not doubt. For if Satan overthrew me, whom the Lord held in such great honour, so that I denied the light of my hope; if he subdued me and persuaded me to flee, as if I had put my trust in a man, what do you expect, you who are new to the faith?

---

[1] Hennecke, *New Testament Apocrypha*, vol. ii, pp. 288–9.

Here, then, we see a pseudonymous sermon attributed to Peter in which he offers himself as example, much in the way people have thought must lie behind the story of the denial in Mark. The exemplary preaching is based in traditions about Peter known to us from the canonical scriptures, just as the exemplary convert Paul in the Pastorals is built out of what we know of Paul's life and apostleship from sources such as Acts and the authentic epistles. Few would argue for the authenticity of words attributed to Peter in this way, and as we have seen, there are real difficulties about the picture of Paul offered in the Pastorals ringing completely true. But both pictures are intelligible as a deliberate attempt to re-present the Apostles in an exemplary light.

Amongst the Apocrypha we also find an epistle to the Laodiceans,[2] purporting to come from Paul:

Paul, an apostle not of men and not through man, but through Jesus Christ, to the brethren who are in Laodicea: Grace to you and peace from God the Father and the Lord Jesus Christ.
I thank Christ in all my prayer that you are steadfast in him and persevering in his works, in expectation of the promise for the day of judgment. And may you not be deceived by the vain talk of some people who tell (you) tales that they may lead you away from the truth of the gospel which is proclaimed by me. And now may God grant that those who come from me for the furtherance of the truth of the Gospel ... may be able to serve and to do good works for the well-being of eternal life.
And now my bonds are manifest, which I suffer in Christ, on account of which I am glad and rejoice. This ministers to me unto eternal salvation, which (itself) is effected through your prayers and by the help of the Holy Spirit, whether it be through life or through death. For my life is in Christ and to die is joy (to me).
And this will his mercy work in you, that you may have the same love and be of one mind. Therefore, beloved, as you have heard in my presence, so hold fast and do in the fear of God, and eternal life will be your portion. For it is God who works in you. And do without hesitation what you do. And for the rest, beloved, rejoice in Christ and beware of those who are out for sordid gain. May all your

---

[2] *Ibid.*, pp. 131–2.

requests be manifest before God, and be ye steadfast in the mind of
Christ. And what is pure, true, proper, just and lovely, do. And what
you have heard and received, hold in your heart and peace will be
with you.
< Salute all the brethren with a holy kiss. > The saints salute you. The
grace of our Lord Jesus Christ be with your spirit. And see this epistle
is read to the Colossians and that of the Colossians among you.

This little document is a kind of pastiche of Pauline phrases
and sentences. It shows that people did try to re-present Paul
in a simplified and summary way, that they wanted to preserve
tradition against misleading tales, that Paul's sufferings were
celebrated, and also by implication here exemplary. The letter
hardly bears comparison with the Pastorals – here indeed is
mediocrity, beside which the Pastorals are fine theology. No
one would attempt to claim authenticity for it, yet it is clear
evidence of an increasing veneration for and use of Paul by
later imitators. Like the first example we looked at, words are
composed in Paul's name, in the first person, and the elements
of the composition are culled from traditions known in the New
Testament.

The most telling of the examples, however, is found in the Acts
of Paul.[3] Here we find a letter written from Corinth to Paul by
Stephanus and the presbyters with him. Stephanus appears in
1 Corinthians, but the names of the presbyters are new –
Daphnus, Eubulus, Theophilus and Xenon. They ask Paul to
help them with a letter or a visit, threatened as they are by
Simon and Cleobius, who pervert the faith. They request that
'while thou art still in the flesh we may hear such things again
from thee', which perhaps betrays that they want the absent
Paul made present despite his death, since they go on, 'For we
believe, as it has been revealed to Theonoe, that the Lord has
delivered thee out of the hand of the lawless one.' One guesses
that Theonoe is meant to be a prophetess, and that the
imagined scenario is that rumours of Paul's death were
countered by a revelation. The letter goes on to specify six

---

[3] *Ibid.*, pp. 352–90.

points of doctrine promulgated by the opposition, words never heard 'either from thee or from the other apostles'. These are: (1) that appeal should not be made to the prophets; (2) that God is not almighty; (3) that there is no resurrection of the flesh; (4) that the human creation is not God's work; (5) that the Lord is not come in the flesh, or born of Mary; (6) that the world is not God's creation, but that of the angels. Here one can recognise teachings similar to those of the gnostics and Marcion in the second century.

Paul 'in affliction' wrote a reply to this letter, sometimes referred to as 3 Corinthians. It is rather longer than the letter already quoted, and will not be reproduced in full. But it is telling for comparative purposes for several reasons. Firstly, the problem of false teachers is similar to that in the Pastorals, and there is some overlap in the kind of doctrines causing trouble. The notion that this is not God's good creation seems to lie behind 1 Tim. 4.1–5, and there seems to be some kind of problem about the resurrection in 2 Tim. 2.18 also. Secondly, the response is to re-tell the biblical story in stereotyped phrases such as would find their place in the Rule of Faith referred to by Irenaeus, Tertullian and Origen as a kind of 'bench-mark' against gnostic speculations, and would eventually find their way into the creeds; in other words, the rehearsal of tradition, and the tradition received from the Apostles in particular, is the counter, as it is beginning to be in the Pastorals. Thirdly, the authority of Paul is presented in exactly the same way as in the Pastorals, through the composition of a letter in his name.

Paul, the prisoner of Jesus Christ, to the brethren in Corinth – greeting! Since I am in many tribulations, I do not wonder that the teachings of the evil one are so quickly gaining ground. For [my] Lord Jesus Christ will quickly come, since he is rejected by those who falsify his words. For I delivered to you in the beginning what I received from the apostles who were before me, who at all times were together with the Lord Jesus Christ, that our Lord Jesus Christ was born of Mary of the seed of David, when the Holy Spirit was sent from heaven by the Father into her, that he might come into this world and redeem all flesh through his own flesh, and that he might raise up from the dead us who are fleshly, even as he has shown himself as our example. And since man was moulded by his Father, for this reason was he sought when he was lost, that he might be quickened by adoption into sonship. For the almighty God, who made heaven and earth, first sent the prophets to the Jews ... But God, the almighty, who is righteous and would not repudiate his own creation, sent the [Holy] Spirit [through fire] into Mary the Galilaean, who believed with all her heart, and she received the Holy Spirit in her womb that Jesus might enter into the world, in order that the evil one might be conquered through the same flesh by which he held sway ... As for those who tell you there is no resurrection of the flesh, for them there is no resurrection who do not believe in him who is thus risen. For indeed, ye men of Corinth, they do not know about the sowing of wheat or the other seeds, that they are cast naked into the ground and when they have perished below are raised again by the will of God in a body and clothed. And not only is the body which was cast [into the earth] raised up, but also abundantly blessed ...[4]

The authority claimed is Paul's, but the emphases are not characteristically Pauline; they are typical of anti-gnostic elements in the Rule of Faith, emphasising the continuity of creation and redemption, the reality of incarnation and resurrection. So here again we have definite evidence of Paul being used as an authority to defend orthodoxy.

As we saw in the opening chapter, the Acts of Paul was written 'out of love for Paul', and the Acts of Paul and Thecla is part of a larger work to which these spurious letters also belong. There is much other evidence that Paul was a controversial figure after his death, leaving a problematic legacy, claimed by both gnostics and orthodox.

That Paul was taken as an authority for gnostic teaching has been shown by Elaine Pagels.[5] Now we have access to gnostic texts, we can see the extent to which Pauline texts are quoted and alluded to, as well as the way in which the inherited Jewish scriptures were re-read in a new way to suit the gnostic outlook. That others in the more orthodox tradition distrusted Paul's letters because they were easily twisted in a gnostic direction is proved by 2 Pet. 3.15–16:

[4] *Ibid.*, pp. 375–6.   [5] Pagels, *The Gnostic Paul.*

Consider our Lord's patience to be salvation, just as our beloved brother Paul also wrote to you according to the wisdom given him. He writes the same way in all his letters, too, speaking on these matters, though there are in them things hard to understand, which the ignorant and unstable distort, as they do the rest of the scriptures also, to their own destruction.

In an important paper on Pauline controversies in post-Pauline churches, C. K. Barrett[6] showed how Paul's teaching had an ambiguous legacy. The Acts picture of Paul, together with the Paul of Ephesians and the Pastorals, offered a 'good' Paul legend to counter the 'bad' Paul legend. The word 'legend' is not meant to suggest that the material was not in the tradition – it was. But it is given particular shape by the exigences of the time. Paul becomes the great missionary Apostle, the Apostle to the Gentiles, with a gospel for the whole world, one who suffered for the sake of the gospel, who was a redeemed persecutor, and the authoritative teacher of the church.

Here, then, is an idealisation of Paul which was natural after his death. It has a basis in the Pauline material. For Paul tells his readers in Corinth and elsewhere (1 Cor. 4.16, 11.1; 1 Thess. 1.6) to be 'imitators of me as I am of Christ'. He argues in 2 Corinthians that sufferings are the mark of the true Apostle. And in Phil. 3.5–11, he portrays himself as the redeemed persecutor. But this tradition is moulded to meet new demands, and particularly the dangerous development of an interpretation of Paul that played into the hands of those who would teach an excessive asceticism or other-worldliness, whether because of gnostic doctrines or not. So we must reopen the question of pseudonymity, but perhaps with a different perspective.

PAUL THE LETTER-WRITER

Letters have conventional openings, and Paul's letters are particularly interesting since they seem to have created a characteristically Christian form of convention, combining the

---

6 Barrett, 'Pauline Controversies in the Post-Pauline Period', pp. 229–45.

usual Greek greeting with the Jewish, and subtly changing *chairein* to *charis* so as to heighten the significance of wishing upon the letter-recipient the grace and peace of God in Christ.[7] These three letters both follow and deviate from the forms found in the other Paulines. Thus Paul is introduced as the letter-writer, and these three letters were successfully passed off as his work, but yet, as with the portrait of Paul examined above, there is something about the presentation of Paul as the letter-writer which does not quite ring true.[8] Let us examine the three greetings:

1 Timothy 1.1–2

Paul, apostle of Christ Jesus according to the command (*epitagē*) of God our Saviour and Christ Jesus our hope, to Timothy, true child in the faith, grace mercy peace from God the Father and Christ Jesus our Lord.

Unusual features are as follows: often Paul calls himself Apostle by the will (*thelēma*) of God, never elsewhere by God's command; God is described as 'our Saviour' (see chapter 3); mercy (*eleos*) is sandwiched between grace and peace. The description of Timothy is also unusual, but since there are no incontestably authentic private or personal letters, we have no real standard of comparison.

2 Timothy 1.1–2

Paul, apostle of Christ Jesus through the will of God, according to the promise of life in Christ Jesus, to Timothy, beloved child, grace mercy peace from God the Father and Christ Jesus our Lord.

Paul's more common usage is produced, Apostle 'according to God's will': this is found in the Corinthian letters, Colossians and Ephesians. But none of these add anything in defence of the claim. Galatians and Romans, however, where Paul's

---

[7] See Judith M. Lieu, '"Grace to you and Peace": The Apostolic Greeting', *BJRL* 68 (1985), 161–78. See also studies of the letter-form: e.g. P. Schubert, *Form and Function of the Pauline Thanksgivings* (Berlin, 1939); W. G. Doty, *Letters in Primitive Christianity* (Philadelphia, 1973).

[8] For another view, see Michael Prior, CM, *Paul the Letter-Writer and the Second Letter to Timothy*, JSNT Supplement Series 23 (Sheffield, 1989). He argues for authenticity, distinguishing between private letters and community letters.

apostleship is contested or needs proving, do elaborate the greeting: Paul is Apostle not from or by human agency, but 'through Jesus Christ and God the Father who raises from the dead', according to Galatians; and according to Romans, Paul was set apart for the gospel, which is then described in a passage often treated as a kind of confession taken over and inserted by Paul to reinforce his claim. The phrase 'according to the promise of life in Christ Jesus' in 2 Timothy is odd, since it has no obvious attachment or purpose, but curiously reflects perhaps the elaborated greetings of Galatians and Romans. We also note the use of 'mercy', again with 'grace' and 'peace'.

Titus 1.1–4

Paul, slave of God, apostle of Jesus Christ, according to the faith of God's elect and knowledge of truth according to piety (*eusebeia*) in hope of eternal life, which the God who cannot lie promised before eternal times, and made manifest his word in his own good time in the *kerygma* (message) with which I was entrusted according to the command (*epitagē*) of our Saviour God, to Titus, true child according to our common faith, grace and peace from God the Father and Christ Jesus our Saviour.

Paul called himself 'slave of Christ Jesus' in writing to the Romans, and though often calling himself Apostle of Christ Jesus, he also insists that he is Apostle by God's will or designation; the language is like Paul's though not exactly paralleled. In the elaborate greeting of Romans we find a confession which might be summed up as 'the faith of God's elect', but Paul has not used such a phrase himself. Still less would he have emphasised knowledge of truth according to piety, characteristic concerns we have already discussed in relation to these letters. Other curious features in this greeting have already been noted in commenting on the greetings in 1 and 2 Timothy: the promise of eternal life seems to dominate the conception of Paul's message, his authority to preach such a message came by God's command, and God is now joined by Christ in being described by the un-Pauline epithet 'Saviour'. With 'grace and peace' we now revert to Paul's usual usage without the 'mercy'.

To sum up, then, there is a heightened sense of Paul's subservience to God, and of his standing at the apex of the theological tradition which these letters represent. Yet the greetings indicate that the 'implied author' of these letters is Paul, and the 'fiction', if fiction it be, is sustained throughout wherever personal details or first-person subjects appear. The oddities in the portrait of Paul with which we are presented in these letters demand that the possibility of fiction be entertained. We have treated these letters as a way of making the absent Paul present, of passing on his authority. This is done by writing in his name. Therefore the widely held conclusion that these letters are pseudonymous seems the most plausible conclusion, and the theological significance of that fact must be addressed.

Pseudonymity is regarded by some as a technique of the deceitful, morally unacceptable and hardly to be countenanced with respect to works regarded as scriptural. In the context of modern presuppositions about authorship, that appears at first sight to be valid, though perhaps it overlooks the not uncommon use of a 'pen-name' by modern authors, a practice which hardly invites the same moral criticism! One might enquire why pen-names are used, but generally we do not speculate – we simply accept the convention. One suspects that George Eliot[9] used the device in order to gain a hearing: in those days a woman would not have achieved access to the right reading public! That may provide a clue: authors are always involved in taking on a certain *persona* which is not their everyday self. Literary critics now speak of the 'implied author' and recognise that that 'person' is not wholly identical with the individual with a particular life-history who happened to write that book at that point. The author's biography does not necessarily illuminate a particular literary work.

If the relationship between author and text is of this complexity, it is hardly surprising that the position is even less clear

---

[9] George Eliot was the pen-name of Mary Anne Evans (1819–80). She translated Strauss' notorious *Life of Jesus* (1846) and Feuerbach's *Essence of Christianity* (1854); but is best known for her novels, including *Adam Bede* (1859), *The Mill on the Floss* (1860), *Silas Marner* (1861), *Felix Holt* (1866) and *Middlemarch* (1871–2).

when one is dealing with texts from a different culture. Not only were the conventions different, but the physical and technological realities of producing written works were dramatically different. It is likely that the extent and practice of literacy have been overestimated, as we noted in an earlier chapter. It is also likely that the circulation of forged documents has been underestimated; in ancient texts, there is not a little talk about guaranteeing authenticity or suspecting that tampering has taken place.

Certainly the extent to which the composition of letters, like that of legal and business documents, would be delegated to 'professional' writers and written in the name of someone who did not actually compose word by word was considerably greater than generally supposed, since tachygraphy (or 'shorthand') was a special skill. The scribe would often 'write up' the letter from skeleton notes. An important analysis of the actual conditions in Paul's time has been undertaken by E. Randolph Richards,[10] who distinguishes between various levels of secretarial activity. One major difficulty is that our best evidence comes from the upper-class correspondence between Cicero and his gentlemanly friends and colleagues, and one wonders how far conclusions can be drawn for artisans with the social status of our Jewish Paul. Nevertheless, there is concrete evidence in the texts that Paul did not physically write his own letters: see Gal. 6.11ff.

Even more important, however, is the point with which this chapter began: Paul's letters, though inspired by a personality with great individuality, were usually in some sense 'community products'. Not only that, but there are many examples of pseudonymous letters circulating in the ancient world which were well-meant attempts to spread the 'truth', taking on the *persona* of a well-known authority. We have noted examples from Christian apocryphal material already. In the Greco-Roman world, it is notorious that the 'historical Pythagoras' is hard to trace, since the quasi-monastic order he founded lasted for many centuries and all the philosophical, mystical and

---

10 E. Randolph Richards, *The Secretary in the Letters of Paul*, Wissenschaftliche Untersuchungen zum Neuen Testament, 2 Reihe, 42 (Tübingen, 1991).

mathematical ideas his followers had were added to the literature of the community and attributed to him. In Jewish literature we not only have a putative parallel in the book of Isaiah, which is more plausibly explained as 'growing' from the activity of a 'school' of Isaiah's disciples over the exilic and post-exilic period than divided into 1, 2 and 3 Isaiah, but there is clear evidence of pseudonymous writing in the Hellenistic period, apocalyptic writing being produced in the name of ancient figures like Enoch, or authoritative figures like Ezra, and Testaments being attributed to the patriarchs.[11]

It is in the light of such parallels that a more positive estimate of the likelihood of pseudonymity has been assumed throughout this study of the theology of these letters. This extends to those passages which in their verisimilitude have often been treated as Pauline fragments.

The fragments hypothesis was advanced by P. N. Harrison.[12] His was the study which did most to convince the English-speaking scholarly world that the letters as they stand cannot be Pauline. His argument was cumulative, drawing on linguistic and historical analysis, as well as theological shifts, to show that stylistically, institutionally, biographically and doctrinally there were enormous difficulties in accepting Paul's authorship. None of these arguments on its own is conclusive, but their cumulative effect, even after certain shifts in detailed historical reconstruction have taken place, remain compelling. But Harrison found certain passages where the vocabulary was not so unusual, and the content particularly personal, which did not seem to fit his hypothesis. These, he suggested, must be authentic fragments.

But that admission in effect weakened his argument. They were precisely those passages which provided verisimilitude, the appearance of being Pauline, by speaking of his imprisonment, his request for books and parchments, and the cloak he left in Troas. There was a larger concentration of such passages in 2 Timothy, their content was not really significant theo-

---

[11] David G. Meade, *Pseudonymity and Canon: An Investigation into the Relationship of Authorship and Authority in Jewish and Earliest Christian Tradition* (Tübingen, 1986).
[12] Harrison, *The Problem of the Pastoral Epistles.*

logically, and many argued that if these so-called fragments were genuine, then there was no reason to doubt the authenticity of the letters as a whole. The changes in style, theological stance and vocabulary could be explained by changes in circumstances, Paul's advancing age, and so on. Now Donelson[13] has argued that the hypothesis of Pauline fragments should be abandoned in the light of the actual practice found in pseudonymous letters of the Hellenistic and Roman periods. Drawing on parallels from the Socratic letters, he proves that personal details were universally used in the attempt to authenticate the material. It is precisely the passages treated as Pauline fragments which are the most compelling evidence for pseudonymity. Nowhere in the authentic letters do we find Paul worrying about missing cloaks, but that is just the kind of detail a forger would invent. In fact, the really important thing about the Pastorals is that they are such skilled forgeries that they were not detected, as other apocryphal material was.

Donelson is not afraid to speak of forgery and deception, and he shows conclusively that people in the ancient world were all too aware of the dangers of such activity, and anxious to develop critical techniques to distinguish genuine works from material masquerading as authentic. He does not, I think, take sufficient account of the psychology of communities passing on tradition. His examples belong to a more elitist literary and philosophical world. The Pastorals, I suggest, emerge from persons who from love of Paul wish to preserve his heritage in the face of distortion. Their use of the techniques of pseudonymous writing is skilled, precisely because so much is at stake. The 'moral' question for us is whether they faithfully guaranteed the Pauline tradition for the future church, or seriously distorted his legacy themselves.[14]

13 Donelson, *Pseudepigraphy and Ethical Argument.*
14 See also Meade, *Pseudonymity and Canon,* e.g. p. 116: 'In other words, in the case of Paul and his churches, the apostolic Gospel (authoritative tradition) is inextricably bound up with the person of Paul himself. Paul is the embodiment of his tradition, and there is little difference between imitating Paul and preserving his tradition.' Also p. 123: 'Behind the Pastorals is a community whose identity was exclusively created and sustained by the figure of Paul. Paul was not only the bearer of the tradition but part of the tradition itself.'

In the light of this study, one might feel disposed to answer such a question relatively favourably, particularly with regard to the 'church orders' of 1 Timothy and Titus. But what do we make of 2 Timothy? It is striking that 2 Timothy differs from the others, at least at first sight. A better case for authenticity can be made for 2 Timothy in terms of vocabulary, style, context and content, yet it is far less clear than in the case of the others what its purpose might be. Recently it has been suggested that this letter should be considered authentic, a fascinating case being made for re-reading it as a plea to Timothy to join Paul quickly because it looks as though he is going to be acquitted and the mission to Spain will be on the agenda after all.[15] This involves some unconventional exegesis, of which much seems quite plausible, but it fails to take account of the many considerations advanced here, or of the evident links between 2 Timothy and the other two letters (e.g. in the greeting, and with respect to the false teachers, etc.). No very satisfactory solution to the purpose of 2 Timothy in relation to the others has been advanced.

It has been noticed, however, that this letter bears some resemblance to a Testament. I would argue that in very general terms the three together form a work which might be described as The Testament of Paul, and in general outline together they have a similar shape to the apocryphal letter to the Laodiceans, which may be seen as a less successful example of a similar work.

The Testaments of the Twelve Patriarchs[16] belong to a loosely defined genre which emerged in the Hellenistic period. As far as we can tell, the Greek version we possess is the original, though the matter is disputed. Despite some evidence of Christian interpolation, the originals would seem to be Jewish in provenance, generally upholding the practice of the

---

[15] Prior, *Paul the Letter-Writer and the Second Letter to Timothy*. Computer analysis by a BD student at Birmingham, Michael Bossingham (unpublished dissertation), also suggests that 2 Timothy stands apart from the others and closer to the authentic letters.

[16] Ed. and trans. H. C. Kee, in Charlesworth, *The Old Testament Pseudepigrapha*, vol. II, pp. 775–828.

law, though with a more universal moralising stance in which
Hellenistic virtues associated with Stoicism figure with some
prominence: integrity, piety, uprightness, generosity, compassion, self-control. Concern with love of money and sexual ethics,
and a certain hostility to women, also feature. An emphasis on
the Two Ways of light and darkness and on the need for
singleness of heart and warnings about the evil deeds to be
practised as the End approaches bear comparison with early
Christian material such as is found in the Apostolic Fathers, as
well as some features of the Pastorals.

But the characteristic of these twelve compositions is that to
each of the twelve sons of Jacob is attributed a dying speech or
Testament. On examination one finds that each has its own
character, and yet they constitute a coherent collection. These
speeches are given verisimilitude by the use and development
of material in the scriptures or in legends and traditions about
each patriarch, the material being characteristically made
exemplary. The exploits of the speaker are celebrated in first-
person form, and sometimes his moral errors are confessed as a
moral lesson – Gad confesses he wanted to kill Joseph out of his
hate and jealousy, and he teaches the evil of hatred. The
overall purpose is to offer sound teaching. In fact, when we
reach the Testament of Joseph, his example also encourages
confidence and hope in God's salvation:

My brothers and my children
Listen to Joseph, the one beloved of Israel . . .
In my life I have seen envy and death.
But I have not gone astray: I continued in the truth of the Lord.
These my brothers hated me, but the Lord loved me.
They wanted to kill me, but the God of my fathers preserved
    me . . .
They sold me into slavery; the Lord of all set me free.
I was overtaken by hunger; the Lord himself fed me . . .
I was alone, and God came to help me.
I was in weakness, and the Lord showed his concern for me . . .
I was in bonds, and he loosed me;
falsely accused, and he testified on my behalf.[17]

---

[17] *Ibid.*, p. 819.

I have deliberately spoken of a loosely defined genre, and I would not think it possible to argue for dependence or even close parallels. But I suggest that these Testaments provide us with the clue to the theological purpose of 2 Timothy, and so also to its place in the three-fold collection. Paul is the exemplary martyr, whose life and death give him the authority to enunciate at his last the appropriate way of life for those who are true to the tradition he initiated, and trust in the Saviour God he preached.

So why in the form of letters rather than a Testament like other Testaments? And why three? Clearly it is part of the verisimilitude for Paul to write letters and so attempt to make his presence felt in his absence. It was appropriate for him to need a cloak, and his book-rolls and note-books, for he was the supreme teacher: did not Thecla don the philosopher's mantle when she sought to follow him? The less successful Laodicean letter sandwiches Paul's testimony through suffering between ethical exhortation, as this three-fold work does. So, I suggest, the purpose of 2 Timothy is to guarantee the Pauline tradition which 1 Timothy has sought to promulgate in the face of distorted versions, and the purpose of Titus is to recapitulate and provide the theological sanctions and slogans that reinforce the message. Hence the cumulative effects we noted in the earlier chapter (chapter 3) in which the theological ideas were examined. The three letters belong together, because only together do they make sense. The heart of their theology is only understood properly if their pseudonymity is acknowledged.

THE RECEPTION OF THE PASTORALS

The provenance of the Pastorals is unknown. Assuming they are pseudonymous, as argued here, they emerge into the life of the church during the second century. Marcion either did not know, or did not care to use, them: they do not appear in his collection. They are unlikely to have been included in the earliest extant papyrus collection of the epistles (Chester Beatty P46). On the other hand, Polycarp clearly did know them – they are closely paralleled, if not quoted, in his letter to

the Philippians. Irenaeus at the end of the second century used
them as authentic in his struggle with Marcion and the gnostics, and so incorporated them in the canonised 'Apostle'. They
appear as part of the Pauline Corpus in the Muratorian
Canon. Subsequently they were used without question.
Their success depended on the pseudonymity being undetec-
ted, as indeed it was. They seem to have had an important
place in the second-century battle for Paul, as we noted
earlier.[18] Neither the gnostic Paul nor the apocalyptic Paul nor
the ascetic Paul was canonised, but the Paul of the Pastorals. It
is fascinating that modern scholarship has skirmished over the
same ground, with Bultmann[19] emphasising the gnostic, Käsemann and Beker[20] the apocalyptic features of Paul's thought.

The success of the Pastorals means that throughout most of
church history Paul has been read through their spectacles.
The great hero, convert and missionary, fount of the tradition,
whom we find depicted here and in Acts, was assumed to be the
author of the other letters. Canonisation of these texts made the
other Pauline texts acceptable, providing a reading which
minimised the gnostic, ascetic and apocalyptic elements which
were too extreme for comfort. The Pastorals were appealed to
to show that Paul could not have meant what in some cases he
seemed to mean. The Pastorals spelt out in practical terms the
consequences for everyday life of becoming a Pauline Christian, and seeking to live a life obedient to God's will without
the Jewish law and its Halakah.

The *Apostolic Constitutions* are not just a compendium of early
collections of canon law, but an important witness to the
development of traditions of 'sound teaching' of the kind promulgated by the Pastorals, often quoting or alluding to their
material. The Homilies of John Chrysostom on these texts
present a picture of Paul as Pastor of his churches which

18 See above, pp. 19–20, 23, 130–3.
19 R. Bultmann, *Theology of the New Testament*, vol. 1 (ET London, 1952).
20 E. Käsemann, *New Testament Questions of Today* (ET London, 1969), especially
'"The Righteousness of God" in Paul', pp. 168–82; and *Perspectives on Paul* (ET
London, 1971). J. C. Beker, *Paul the Apostle: The Triumph of God in Life and Thought*
(Edinburgh, 1989, first published Philadelphia, 1980).

continued the process of domesticating Paul on the basis of the Pastorals for church tradition and its clerical orders. By the time of the Reformation, these documents provided the scriptural basis for attempting to reform the clerical orders, though the primacy of the doctrine of justification by faith, believed from the time of the Reformers to be Paul's revolutionary and characteristic teaching, would eventually sow the seeds of doubt about their Pauline authorship, since on this issue they seemed not to uphold the Pauline tradition with due clarity.

When it comes to our own appropriation of the Pastorals, we have to reckon both with the history of these texts in the reception of Paul and with the issues raised by Paul being fictionally portrayed as the writer of these letters. What are the consequences of challenging the identity of the implied author, and indeed the implied readers, for our reading of these texts as canonical scripture? To such questions we turn in the final chapter.

CHAPTER 7

The Pastorals as scripture

Paul has been mediated to the church through the tradition of the Pastorals, and the Pastorals have for most of church history been part of the canon of scripture. It is one thing to investigate their origins and their theological interpretation as historical documents; it is another to move from exegesis to appropriation. This we will now attempt.

THE PROBLEM OF THE PASTORALS AS CANONICAL SCRIPTURE

The problem of the Pastorals has been conceived by New Testament critics in the following terms: (1) They are pedestrian, unimaginative, a sad falling away from the greatness and vitality of Paul, lacking in engagement with the issues and real argument with the opponents, doctrinally and stylistically weak and bland. (2) They reflect a 'bourgeois' lifestyle of respectability, rather than radical commitment, or engagement with the world – Christians are losing their cutting-edge in society. (3) They are concerned with organisation rather than theology. (4) They are collections of random thoughts and instructions lacking coherence. Compared with Pauline and Johannine theology they are quite simply inferior.

Many of these judgments have been contested in recent literature. In his commentary, Norbert Brox accepted that the Pastorals are later, but insisted that that does not mean inferior – they provided the consolidation needed at the time, and carried the Pauline tradition forward into a new situation.[1]

[1] Brox, *Die Pastoralbriefe.*

145

Howard Marshall has pursued these ideas in his Peake lecture,[2] and developed the notion that the Pastorals creatively apply, re-use and adapt the key Pauline ideas within a new situation. The discussions found in this book follow a similar general line. A new convergence of scholarly work is arriving at a more positive estimate of the value of the Pastorals over against the older view, which arose largely from the historical judgment that these texts were pseudonymous and secondary. There is encouraging reassessment of the denigratory views once standard, views which reflected unfortunate Protestant prejudices against 'early catholicism', depended on the modern interest in the creative individual, so implying standards of judgment which cannot be regarded as appropriate, and reinforced the tendency to look for a canon within the canon rather than seeking a hermeneutic for each and every text which has become part of the canonical literature.

The problem of the Pastorals as part of the canon, however, goes far deeper than this. It may be put quite sharply, especially but not only by feminist theologians. As scripture, the Pastorals have shaped a world in which women and others have been subordinated and devalued on the authority of God's Word. As we have seen, the Pastorals encourage a hierarchical view of the way things are. Not only have they appeared to establish a clerical hierarchy, though this has been differently interpreted by Protestant and Catholic exegetes, but their actual text reinforces patriarchal hierarchy in family, society and church, apparently providing warrant for this from scripture. Such texts contained in a sacred authoritative canon cannot but become 'texts of terror'[3] in a democratic society which views the position of women, lay people, servants, slaves, etc. in a totally different light. Taken at face value they appear to perpetuate with the authority of God patterns

---

[2] I. Howard Marshall, '"Sometimes only Orthodox" – Is there More to the Pastoral Epistles?', A. S. Peake Memorial Lecture 1992, to be published in the *Epworth Review*.

[3] This phrase is the title of a feminist study of scripture: Phyllis Trible, *Texts of Terror: Literary and Feminist Readings of Biblical Narratives* (Philadelphia, 1984).

of relationship which are no longer acceptable, and may be regarded as opposed to the fundamental outlook of the Christian tradition, even of Paul himself in his better moments (e.g. Gal. 3.28).

But the difficulties go even deeper. It has been said that monotheism naturally allies itself with monarchy, and everything in these letters points in that direction. The very nature and being of God is conceived as the great imperial power, benevolent rather than tyrannical, it is true, effecting salvation rather than oppression, and yet without question at the apex of a hierarchy, demanding obedience from his subjects, a majestic, male superpower, access to whom comes through his servants and officials. Everything comes from the top down. The saving grace of such a figure might well be spurned these days as patronising charity! The theology of the Pastorals presents us with a whole culture of subordination. The Roman imperial system has been sacralised. No matter how kindly the Supreme Ruler be presented, an inherently oppressive social order has been projected onto the heavens. The problems of this picture are compounded by a view of 'teaching' which we might well characterise as oppressively dogmatic and authoritative, an educative process integrated into this monarchical authority-structure, with no sense of training a person to be free and independent, creative, or autonomous in taking responsibility for his or her own actions.

So what can we do in a modern democratic system but reject texts which are clearly out-dated and inappropriate? But to do that is to challenge the deep instinct and tradition of the church that these texts belong to the canon of scripture, that they are in some sense sacred and authoritative, and appropriately read in a liturgical context. What can we make of this situation? How can we be true to ourselves, to our deepest social and moral commitments, while remaining true to the Christian tradition?

Some will conclude that this is impossible, and that the rest of this chapter is special pleading. Others may wish to pursue the following lines of thought further.

HERMENEUTICS AND THE ETHICS OF READING

In recent years there has been increasing interest in the hermeneutical question concerning present reading and appropriation of texts from the past. Even if 'assured results' of historical criticism were obtainable, and increasingly this is put in question as we realise how our own concerns and presuppositions inevitably affect even the most determined effort at objective exegesis, purely historical reading runs the risk of being 'archaeological' and not producing any hermeneutic. At the same time, literary theory has been challenging the notion that knowledge of the author's biography or situation gives access to the meaning of a text. Meaning is not confined to the conscious intention of the author, but particularly in the case of poetry, and in practice in the case of all texts, meaning may transcend both the author and his or her time. Indeed, in the ancient and medieval worlds, the artefact was more important than the craftsman, who was usually anonymous. Gradually a shift has taken place to concentrating on the reader, and the way a text is read.[4]

The problem with the reader response approach, however, is that it can seem to become entirely subjective. The many different readings, Freudian, Marxist, feminist, etc., may fit the relativism and pluralism of modern culture, but hardly allow the reader to do justice to the text's 'otherness' and autonomy. The sense of being addressed, of the moral necessity to endeavour to understand what is being communicated and not simply get out of the text what one is looking for, is eroded. For readers of texts which have scriptural status, the dangers of projecting onto scripture one's own desires and needs, finding confirmation of one's own prejudices, are compounded. It is this kind of problem which raises the question of 'ethical reading'.

---

[4] Werner G. Jeanrond, in *Text and Interpretation as Categories of Theological Thinking* (ET Thomas J. Wilson, Dublin, 1988), discusses reader response theories, examining the work of Wolfgang Iser and Stanley Fish. For a survey of current literary theory, see William Ray, *Literary Meaning: From Phenomenology to Deconstruction* (Oxford, 1984).

Hermeneutical discussion[5] tended to repudiate the notion that a 'dialogue' is possible with a text: the writing–reading relationship is not the same as the speaking–hearing one, if only because direct questioning about meaning is rendered impossible. Once written, the author loses control over the text. Yet readers need to 'enter the world of the text', in some sense submit to what is there, and allow the possibility of change, of viewing the world they inhabit in a different light as a result of reading the text, perhaps changing their own behaviour. They also need to exercise a 'hermeneutic of suspicion' to avoid being taken in or taken over by the text inappropriately.

This kind of stance is not unlike that of an ethical reading which takes with proper seriousness the need to be true both to the text and to oneself. In reaction against subjectivism, the point has been made that a reader has a moral responsibility to the text. It should be received with courtesy and welcome. A kind of dialogical relationship is being re-established, one in which the two parties to a kind of conversation are recognisably different, and in which the aim is to do justice to both sides.[6]

These theoretical developments in fact encourage both a historical reading and a reading of the text as scripture, the latter demanding respect and attention, the former appropriate distance. Just as legal documents need constant reinterpretation as they are applied to new cases and new situations, or indeed as the moral sensibilities of a society develop (e.g. with respect to capital punishment), so a sacred text requires appropriate critical reading if its meaning is to be discerned in new contexts. What we need to do is to look for the 'spirit' of the text as it relates to the specific particularities of the historical moment of its production. Thus I would argue that there are important directions mapped for the Christian tradi-

---

[5] This paragraph is a highly condensed summary of a major area of discussion. It reflects in particular the work of Paul Ricœur. Readers are referred to Jeanrond, *Text and Interpretation as Categories of Theological Thinking*, and the bibliography offered and surveyed in that work. He discusses Ricœur, pp. 37–63.

[6] Frances Young, 'The Pastoral Epistles and the Ethics of Reading', *JSNT* 45 (1992) 105–20.

tion in these letters, and it is these directions that remain telling even if certain specific prescriptions, arguments and values may be subject to cultural revision. Some of these potential signposts are the better illuminated by the kind of historical theology we have been engaged in in the course of this book, as will become clear as this final chapter proceeds.

REVELATION AND PARTICULARITY

As hinted already at the beginning of this book, this general hermeneutical stance is, I suggest, profoundly consonant with the incarnational structure of Christian theology, a structure itself based upon the Word of God in scripture, and embodied in the Pastoral epistles themselves.

Such a large claim demands explanation and justification. The fact is that scripture is a diverse collection of writings in a variety of genres and is not self-explanatory, not even as a complete canon.[7] In the earliest period of developing Christian consciousness when the canon was itself still in process of formation, it was precisely in contention with gnostics that the 'over-arching story' of the Bible was summarised in a creed-like Canon of Truth in order to ensure that the kernel of the faith, in the light of which the manifold scriptures were to be read, should be clarified. That kernel was essentially a narrative, in which the eternal Creator God brought the universe into being, and then entered into relationship with the particularities of its history.

As in any relationship, there were stages, specific moments of engagement. God accommodated the divine communication to the language of limited human historical persons such as the prophets and their hearers. The divine self was accommodated to the limitations of a particular historical person in a particular historical situation. For communication was possible in no other way. The particular mediates the eternal. That is not exactly the kind of language the ancient church used, but it

---

[7] Despite the efforts of canon-criticism, notably of B. S. Childs, both in his work on the Old Testament as canon and in *The New Testament as Canon: An Introduction* (London, 1984).

expresses the spirit of their rejection of docetism and of a gnostic spirituality which denied the importance of the material creation as the medium of God's activity. The very notion of incarnation demands that justice be done to the specific particularities of a text earthed in a historical and cultural situation, and justice can only be done to these particularities by recognising their essential incommensurability – no other human historical moment is exactly the same. Revelation takes place not despite the changes and chances of this life, but in and through them.

In their insistence upon the goodness of created things, in their concern with everyday decent living, in their very 'inculturation' of the gospel, the Pastorals themselves teach the sacredness of the particular, and so invite us to discern what, if that was the revelation for them, the revelation might now be for us, particularly the revelation of the right way of life for a Christian in society. This means we have to read the Pastorals as texts with 'Two Natures', eternal and particular, divine and human.[8] These are not readily distinguishable. The text cannot simply be carved up into bits which are only of historical interest and bits which remain true in all times. For 'incarnation' is union, the human and historical is the medium of the transcendent and eternal. It is precisely as they grapple with specific challenges then that the Pastorals point the way for others who would be true to their tradition as they grapple with new and different challenges now. And interestingly enough, the Pastorals themselves were struggling to do justice to a tradition they had inherited, which was in contention, from which problematic deductions were being made, and that is not unlike the position in which modern interpreters find themselves.

IN THE WORLD BUT NOT OF THE WORLD?

The Pastorals have been criticised for their accommodation to the world. Paul's radical and explosive originality has been

---

[8] See further my book *The Art of Performance* (London, 1990).

domesticated, it is said.[9] The ethic is 'bourgeois': here is a comfortable Christianity of good works, 'godliness with contentment' (1 Tim. 6.6).

If valid, and there have been a number of studies suggesting on several grounds that it is hardly fair,[10] such a criticism fails to take account of the sacredness of the ordinary and the dangers of radicalism. The context of the Pastorals would appear to be reaction against the kind of radicalism that rejects the world and its ties. To live as if heaven were already here, without any appreciation of the material world, its food and wine, its social and community structures, is treated as flouting the goodness of the Creator God. Other kinds of radicalism are around in the modern church. The stance of the Pastorals would appear to be that, although there is a point at which loyalty to Christ demands acceptance of persecution, the shame of criminal charges, opposition to the powers that be, nevertheless for most people most of the time, loyalty to Christ is expressed in everyday living according to the highest, indeed universal, human values of peace, integrity, thankfulness and respect for the 'given-ness' of life, loyalty to others and to the truth, generosity and the obligations of love in community. Such might be our way of talking about 'piety', righteousness and faith.

There are few places in the New Testament which encourage the kind of radicalism that seeks to establish the kingdom of God by human sacrifice or effort – most were awaiting the End of the World in God's good time, and urge the followers of Jesus to live as if the kingdom were already a reality. Paul seems to have thought that what he was doing was establishing in each locality a kind of nucleus of God's kingdom in which the divine Spirit produced a harvest of love, joy, peace,

---

[9] Hanson wrote: 'If they are Pauline, they represent a dismal conclusion to Paul's writings; if they are post-Pauline, they are an admirable and indispensable illustration of the state of the church at the end of the first century' (*Studies in the Pastoral Epistles*, p. 120). This sums up the attitude of Dibelius–Conzelmann and subsequent commentators who have taken the letters as pseudonymous. As we have seen, recent work has criticised this general position: see above, pp. 24–5, 33, 74, 138–9.

[10] Reference has been made to Schwartz, Towner, Donelson, Kidd, etc. See above, pp. 33ff., 74, 138–9.

patience, kindness, goodness, faithfulness, gentleness and self-control (Gal. 5.22). The Pastorals reinforce this 'quietism' against the more radical ascetics or gnostics. Is there not a place for encouraging modern Christians to seek to live according to these 'heart' values within their particular context, rather than exhorting everyone to abandon the situation in which they find themselves and seek radical change? Society requires a certain stability, public life a tradition of faithful service, peace a tradition of law and order. Radicals are two-a-penny; saints are not. Should not the Christian calling be to saintliness? And if saintliness seems unexciting, even conventional, then maybe that is an affirmation of the essential goodness of God's world, despite the fact that everyone falls short of the divine glory.

In a strange kind of way, the Pastorals encourage not only social responsibility but also a kind of catholic sectarianism. Simply because God is Creator of the universe, the outlook cannot but be catholic, an insistence on public, universal truth against esoteric speculation, a baptising of the social order recognising that it has its source in God's order. Yet this minority group with its specific commitment to Christ remains ready to confront, to be 'cut off' as a distinct 'sect' with a distinct view of the way the world is and the way the world should be. To be true to this perspective requires not the reproduction of the Pastorals' particular ethical maxims so much as a parallel movement to embrace what is universally true and good in the particular social and cultural context in which we find ourselves, while reserving the right to be critical, to jettison value-systems that undermine the moral qualities that are common to decent human life and the gospel. For such value-systems are a corruption of goodness, and so idolatry, Caesar-worship, sin.

At this point it becomes important to note again that the Pastorals are not about functions but about character. For all the appeal to these texts to validate particular forms of clerical ministry, they give us precious little on which to base church order. What they do tell us is something about the character of the Christian, whatever his or her calling – for bishop, deacon, presbyter and widow are expected to be persons with similar qualities. The 'man of God' addressed is not 'male' but 'human' (*anthrōpos*), and time and again it is irrelevant precisely who is being addressed. The character of the Christian, especially but not solely the Christian in a leadership position, should evidence qualities which largely remain the key to everyday Christian living whatever the social and cultural context or the particular practical actions in which those qualities are expressed. And those qualities are often those recognised by the 'good man', or indeed woman, of any philosophy or background.

The gospel needs to be 'inculturated'. We need some concept of what an everyday Christianity might look like in a pluralist world, and how Christians are to live responsibly as a committed minority in society. The Pastorals may perhaps provide some guidelines for the post-Christian world, not in a direct way, but certainly through demonstrating how some early Christian communities, in days before being a Christian was socially acceptable, sought to live out their faith in a particular historical and cultural environment.

THE FREEDOM OF CONSTRAINT

There is, of course, a danger of these texts encouraging subordinates to sacrifice their own interests in humble submission to those above them. In the twentieth century, we have grown beyond approval of slavery, and even of service in the old literal sense of someone being employed to wait on someone else and live in obedience to and dependency upon them. Many wish that similar progress had been made in recognising the equal value of women and children, as well as minorities and exploited low-paid workers, often predictably found in the so-called 'service industries'. In such a climate, the hierarchical assumptions of the Pastorals are uncongenial to many, though some fundamentalists and traditionalists may exploit them to consolidate their position, particularly as male teachers or priests.

We should not overlook the fact, however, that in these texts those with power are also under authority, and are expected to exercise their power not only responsibly, but with respect for those who are at their service. Nor should we imagine that our own society escapes being hierarchical. By pretending it should not be, we fail to establish appropriate ways of dealing with relationships which necessarily are of a hierarchical kind. Our own society in practice recognises the need to spell out in legal terms the mutual respect for one another's rights required by employer and employee, for example. We need appropriate ethical norms for the relationship between husband and wife, parent and child, pastor and people. The Pauline letters 'baptise' the norms of the Greco-Roman world. Given the breakdown of norms in our society, could we not forge new ones from the old material, accepting the validity of those qualities which make up Christian character, while discovering new ways of exercising those qualities in practice?

Until something like this is managed, it will probably not be possible for the church to accommodate its inherited hierarchical norms to the modern world, nor will the radical, world-changing edge of the gospel be heard. The church seeks to live as a community, indeed as God's family or household, and such relationships cannot be developed without the members accepting obligations and restraints in respect for one another. There are real dangers in freedom, in individual rights without duties and obligations. No one is free unless all are free; all cannot be free through a free-for-all. In any community life, people learn not only give-and-take, but repentance and forgiveness, not only compromise, but self-acceptance and self-affirmation, not only acceptance of discipline and criticism, but also humility rather than humiliation through discovering that service is perfect freedom, that paradoxically self-denial may be self-fulfilment through being 'for' others. To re-read the emphasis on submission in the Pastorals in terms of what is required of all, whether high or lowly, in order that community may flourish is to discover how the Christian character they encourage may be appropriately developed in a different cultural setting.

Our global village needs a demonstration of such community. The way in which a visionary hermeneutic of the ethics of the Pastorals might be constructed is perhaps indicated by the interesting use of the 'household' metaphor in Konrad Raiser's developing reflection on the ecumenical process. Discerning what he calls a 'paradigm shift in the ecumenical movement',[11] he characterises its undergirding theology in the post-war, post-colonial period as 'Christocentric universalism', and recognises that the new situation of religious pluralism, ecological anxieties and the emerging need to affirm diversities requires a new theological paradigm. He speaks of a move from the trumphalism of the Lordship of Christ to the image of the 'household of life', with a theocentric rather than Christocentric focus. The hierarchical assumptions of the Pastorals demonstrate that that could turn out not to be as radical a move as Raiser hopes. On the other hand, he outlines a possible reminting of the metaphor in terms of modern understanding of a family community living together, with its personal differences respected and contained. The 'household of life' signifies a global familial community keeping its house in order and its home fit to live in. This ecumenical vision has to burst the bounds of sectarianism and embrace the pluralism not only of Christianity but of humanity.

Such appropriation of the key images and values of the Pastorals should also help to illuminate what true Christian ministry is. Any community needs its corporate memory; any community needs structure and the exercise of leadership. But any authority the authorised bearer of the tradition may claim, any power the leader and administrator may acquire, all is ultimately for the sake of service to the community. Although the Pastorals lack reference to the exemplary sacrifice of Christ, the fountain of their tradition did not: for Paul, the imitation of Christ's acceptance of suffering for the sake of his mission lay at the heart of Christian ministry, indeed gave Paul his credentials (2 Corinthians). The Pastorals attempt to spell out the character which would result from having 'this mind in you which was in Christ Jesus' (Phil. 2.5).

---

[11] Konrad Raiser, *Ecumenism in Transition. A Paradigm Shift in the Ecumenical Movement?*, ET Tony Coates (Geneva, 1991).

If the church had taken seriously its own critique of the world's success-values, its practical expression of hierarchical authority would have been deeply modified. The Pastorals bear witness to the perennial strains occasioned by the fact that the gospel challenges human assumptions about status and power. What is remarkable in these texts is the extent to which social norms were modified rather than the degree to which they were accepted without challenge. In significant ways, the Christianising of the household table did not leave it the same as before. Accepting the goodness of the social order does not mean selling out to it. Maybe now it is necessary both to challenge hierarchical assumptions in the name of Christ who was the servant of all, and to recall those who would enter his community to the necessity of accepting restraints on their freedom for the sake of all. In a world in which so many claim their 'rights', such suggestions are not likely to be popular, and it must be stressed that this is no plea for unquestioning acceptance of the norms advanced in these letters. But it is worth considering whether life in community does not demand some kind of submission, constraint and service, and whether such service may not after all be perfect freedom.

But if we are to attempt to suggest that the Christian life is a life of service, does that mean that God is the ultimate dictator to be given unquestioning obedience? The theology of the Pastorals at first sight comes dangerously near to suggesting that, and it is to this that we must now turn.

GOD IN THE PASTORALS

Of course in a world of Caesar-worship, it was preferable to owe allegiance to the one true God of the universe. That the Pastorals have that perspective is a fact we cannot change. The question is does it disqualify us from reading and attending to their theology?

There are many even in our democratic society who continue to use the language of God's kingdom without noticing the cultural difficulties, and there are many who sing with abandon about worshipping God's Majesty. For such people, the depiction of an imperial God communicating through a mediator, Jesus Christ, presents no difficulty. They need an authority, and better it be divine than some tyrannical human institution. However, some voices are beginning to challenge these usages, with justification, just as Raiser has challenged the triumphalist theology of Christ's Lordship. There is in the Christian tradition itself a critique of the way of power, for Jesus took the way of the servant, and Jesus is taken to represent the way of God's regime. Can the theology of the Pastorals be understood to have within it the seeds of a critique of its own hierarchical perspective? Or, alternatively, is a response of awe, respect and humility appropriate to the human condition, a quality which the church needs to oppose to the 'autonomy' of modernism? Such questions need addressing.

The patience of the Saviour, the goodwill of the universal God towards the whole of the creation, and the 'otherness', the holiness, of this transcendent source of all things are important aspects of the description of the great King of Kings and Lord of Lords found in the Pastorals. This is a King of grace, mercy and peace, not one who simply exercises unlimited power. The emphasis is on the kindness and love of our Saviour God. But the picture remains one of an ideal benevolence exercised by a ruler, an ideal reflecting the perfect social order envisaged in the ancient world, in which dependants returned homage for benefits in a reciprocal relationship of grace and favour on the one hand and thanksgiving and honour on the other. A theological ethic of obedience, submission and service is grounded in a lordly God, however much God is at the service of those under his rule. Ultimately there will be divine judgment, not divine submission. It is difficult to argue that the Pastorals contain the seeds of a serious critique of a theology of power and dominance.

The question is, however, whether belief in God does not necessitate a recognition of human contingency, and whether spirituality, like membership of community, does not demand a recognition of the need for individual constraint, humble submission to a transcendent reality, with the confidence and assurance that the character of that immortal, invisible holiness is such that awe and respect may also be love and thankfulness. Is it not true that judgment is part of the structure of genuine love, the demand that the 'other' become what he or she perfectly is? Do we not find ourselves as we lose ourselves in something much bigger than ourselves? For in receiving the stature of Christ we are enabled to stand tall, and in living for him, we find our true humanity. Maybe the Pastorals fall short of spelling this out, but we might see it as an implicate of the Pauline tradition as expressed in Gal. 2.20 and 3.26–8, and so discern in the encouragement to humility found in the Pastorals the seeds of such a spirituality.

Indeed, appropriate receptivity would seem to be essential both for spirituality and for 'good work'. Too easily the charity of the rich and powerful can become patronising, unless it is grounded in the sense that everything comes from God, 'who richly provides everything' (1 Tim. 6.17). Such a perception makes possessiveness impossible, and sharing imperative. Even the mutual reciprocity of giving and receiving has an important moral and spiritual dimension: for dignity and respect are accorded to those from whom we receive, not to those we patronise.

Perhaps the Pastorals, by sharpening up the issues for us, help us to discern what appropriate subordination might be, and encourage us to discover in our context how to live out the goal of Christian teaching. For that goal is love, love which issues from a pure heart, a good conscience and unfeigned loyalty (1 Tim. 1.5). This goal is so far-reaching that legal or moral codes cannot touch it. Getting the priorities right means submission to the way of the servant, Christ, and finding right relationships within the community of God's household. People who fail to get these priorites right make shipwreck of the faith. Living out these priorities means putting prayer and worship first, and such worship must be appropriate to current social norms and decency. Faith, love, holiness and self-restraint are the qualities produced by following God's way, and it is important that church leaders demonstrate as well as teach these qualities.

Of course there will be some radicals who cannot accept the

basic goodness of God's ordering of the world, and demand extreme sacrifices for the sake of the gospel. But the truth lies in sanctifying the ordinary things of life, and hoping in God alone for the future. Scripture always provides a guide, but also needs respectful interpretation. The tradition is entrusted to the church and its leaders, so proper order is important. The crucial thing, however, is the gospel of God's grace seen in the appearance of Jesus Christ, which makes it possible for us to abandon the self-seeking ways of the world and learn the way of God, a way that fosters community and respect for one another. In no way have we deserved God's grace and mercy, but the divine generosity has poured out the Spirit, bringing the possibility of life and love. That is what determines Christian priorities.

Something like the last two paragraphs summarises the 'spirit' or 'heart' of the Pastoral epistles, hard though it is to distinguish the 'eternal truths' from the particular historical dress in which they are found. The question for modern Christians is how in practice such teaching might be embodied in the particularities of our own society and culture.

THE ULTIMATE GOAL

As we have seen, the Pastorals are preoccupied with 'sound teaching', but they offer very little doctrine, very little moral law. What they do is to set up an appropriate community structure within which the tradition received from Paul can be safeguarded against speculative interpretation, and by word, precept and example taught and learnt. The teaching is thus embodied in the people. It is not spelt out credally, it is presupposed, alluded to, taken for granted. It is characterised through the repetition of those Christian qualities of life expected of people in leadership positions, together with a placing of the scriptures at the core of the pursuit of holiness.

If this is truly the character of the Pastorals, then they leave open the question of how a properly inculturated Christian community will embody Christian character and safeguard the tradition in a different environment. They present us not just with a model but with a challenge. The challenge is to find the appropriate way of reclaiming the church's self-consciousness of itself as a learning community, centred on a Holy Book, with education for the whole of life, moral, physical and spiritual at its heart.

And the ultimate goal of this educative process? The Pastorals would look to eternal life as the outcome. Salvation, as we have seen, is about the gift and attainment of that perfection which is God's will for humanity, which will inherit eternal life, receive the crown of righteousness and share in eternal glory. This hope is perhaps the final challenge of these epistles to an age which dare not hope beyond the present order.

Annotated bibliography

COMMENTARIES

Commentaries on the Pastorals divide themselves into those defending Pauline authorship and those arguing for authenticity. The most distinguished of the latter are J. N. D. Kelly and George W. Knight III, Knight providing a large and detailed exegesis of the Greek text, Kelly following the pattern of the Black's Commentaries, in which the commentator provides his own translation and writes for the general reader as well as the specialist.

Dibelius–Conzelmann provide much Greek material illustrating the Hellenistic character of the letters. It is particularly helpful that this classic treatment of these letters as pseudonymous and reflecting the 'bourgeois', 'early catholic' stage of development in the early church is available in English. Barrett and Houlden are relatively brief; Scott and Hanson somewhat larger. These provide useful material for the student, and all are written from the perspective of pseudonymity.

Commentaries available in English are referred to in the footnotes by author(s), and publication details are listed below in alphabetical order.

Barrett, C. K. *The Pastoral Epistles*, New Clarendon Bible, Oxford, 1963.
Dibelius–Conzelmann: Dibelius, Martin and Conzelmann, Hans *The Pastoral Epistles*, ET Philip Buttolph and Adela Yarbro, in *Hermeneia – A Critical and Historical Commentary on the Bible*, Philadelphia, 1972.
Hanson, A. T. *The Pastoral Epistles*, The New Century Bible Commentary, Grand Rapids and London, 1982.
Houlden, J. L. *The Pastoral Epistles*, first published by Penguin, London, 1976; republished in TPI New Testament Commentaries, London and Philadelphia, 1989.

Kelly, J. N. D. *The Pastoral Epistles*, Black's New Testament Commentaries, London, 1963.

Knight, III, George W. *The Pastoral Epistles: A Commentary on the Greek Text*. The New International Greek Testament Commentary, Grand Rapids and Carlisle, 1992.

Scott, E. F. *The Pastoral Epistles*, The Moffatt New Testament Commentary, London, 1936.

STUDIES

Studies have also tended to focus on the question of authenticity, though this is now changing. The classic study arguing pseudonymity, with Pauline fragments, was
P. N. Harrison, *The Problem of the Pastoral Epistles*, Oxford, 1921.
Another with a similar perspective was
A. T. Hanson, *Studies in the Pastoral Epistles*, London, 1968.

On the general question of pseudonymity, one classic article is
K. Aland, 'The Problem of Anonymity and Pseudonymity in Christian Literature of the First Two Centuries', *JTS* 12 (1961), 39ff.

D. G. Meade, *Pseudonymity and Canon: An Investigation into the Relationship of Authorship and Authority in Jewish and Earliest Christian Tradition*, WUNT, Tübingen, 1986, is a comprehensive study of the issues, with many good points about the Pastorals and the Pauline tradition.

The connections between pseudonymity and the ethical and theological content of these epistles should also be explored in
Lewis R. Donelson, *Pseudepigraphy and Ethical Argument in the Pastoral Epistles*, *HUT* 22, Tübingen, 1986.

On the social background, the work of American scholars has been particularly important. An excellent general book is
Wayne Meeks, *The First Urban Christians. The Social World of the Apostle Paul*, London, 1983.

Abraham J. Malherbe, *Social Aspects of Early Christianity*, Philadelphia, 1983, not only surveys the then situation in sociological approaches to the New Testament, but has significant chapters on house-churches and hospitality. His important work connecting Paul, and then the Pastorals, with the cultural background of popular philosophers, especially the Cynics, has been collected and published in
Paul and the Popular Philosophers, Minneapolis, 1989.

Useful background will also be found in

Robert Banks, *Paul's Idea of Community: The Early House Churches in their Historical Setting*, Grand Rapids, 1980; and
Ernest Best, *Paul and his Converts*, Edinburgh, 1988.

Although he frequently takes his argument further than is really convincing,
Bruce Malina, *The New Testament World: Insights from Cultural Anthropology*, London, 1983, is often challenging and illuminating from the point of view of entering a world 'constructed' from a very different mind-set from our own.

A couple of theses published in the SBL Dissertation series are particularly pertinent:
David C. Verner, *The Household of God: The Social World of the Pastoral Epistles*, SBL Dissertation Series 71, Chico, CA, 1983.
Reggie M. Kidd, *Wealth and Beneficence in the Pastoral Epistles: A 'Bourgeois' Form of Early Christianity?*, SBL Dissertation Series 122, Atlanta, GA, 1990.

On the development of the Pauline churches and the Pauline tradition, the following studies have influenced this work, though they are not convincing in every respect:
D. R. MacDonald, *The Legend and the Apostle: The Battle for Paul in Story and Canon*, Philadephia, 1983.
Margaret Y. MacDonald, *The Pauline Churches: A Socio-historical Study of Institutionalization in the Pauline and Deutero-Pauline Writings*, SNTS Monograph Series, Cambridge, 1988.
Elaine Pagels, *The Gnostic Paul: Gnostic Exegesis of the Pauline Letters*, Philadelphia, 1975, 1992.

On the theology of the Pastorals, see
Philip H. Towner, *The Goal of our Instruction: The Structure of Theology and Ethics in the Pastoral Epistles*, JSNTS Monograph Series 34, Sheffield, JSOT Press, 1989. This provides a study of key concepts, taking account of work such as that of Donelson (listed above).

On church order, the classic studies are reviewed by
James Tunstead Burtchaell, *From Synagogue to Church: Public Services and Offices in the Earliest Christian Communities*, Cambridge, 1992; his critical survey and fresh approach reflect current interest in the continuities and discontinuities between Christian sectarians and the Jewish community.

Index of references

Index of subjects

advent 64
Alexander 6, 71, 78
Antioch 12, 15, 126
apocalypse 15–16, 40, 95, 118, 143
apocrypha
  Acts of Paul 13–16, 23, 40, 87, 129,
    132, 133
  Acts of Paul and Thecla, 14, 17, 19,
    118, 132
  Acts of Peter, 128
  New Testament 89
  3 Corinthians 131
Apostolic Fathers 42–5, 90, 141
Aristides, Aelius 17
ascension 68
asceticism 6, 10, 13–18, 36, 38, 118,
  120
Asia, province of 125
Athens 26
authorship 122
  of Letters 2–3, 63, 133–6, 137–42, 144

baptism 70
Beatitudes 14
benefactors 34, 101
bishops 12, 43, 52, 90, 91, 97, 153 *see also*
  episkopos

canonical status 75, 143, 145–6
catholicism, early 74, 96, 97, 146
celibacy 15, 36, 43, 117–20
Celsus 16–17
Cerinthus 11–12
character, qualities of 32
charisma 69
chastity 6, 13, 14
child-bearing 36–7, 70
Christ
  as Lord 59, 63, 65, 67

the mediator 62–3
church
  as teacher 84
  house-churches 18–19, 34, 35, 83,
    109
Chrysostom, Dio 85
Chrysostom, John 116, 143–4
citizenship 65
Clement 43–4, 65, 91, 104
codes, household 32–3, 39, 98–9
community manuals 4
conduct 32–4
conformity, social 41
converts
  Jewish 8, 10, 27
  Paul's 86, 89, 98, 122
Corinth 11, 43, 108, 130–1
covenant, new 124
creation 38, 66, 96
Creator God 38, 50, 58, 72, 152–3
Crete 9, 104
Cynics 17, 85–8, 100, 112

date of Pastorals 3, 11–12, 15, 22–3
deacons 19, 43, 97, 153 *see also diakonai*
Decalogue 26
delegates of God 67, 85, 90, 95
diakonai 98–9, 105, 110, 111–14, 123 *see*
  also deacons
Didachē 4, 33
didaskalia 75, 77
discipleship 58
doxology 48, 60–1, 96

enkrateia 7, 13, 32, 119
Ephesus 9, 11, 64
epiphany 58, 63–4, 65, 70, 126
episkopoi 32, 33, 37, 55, 89, 98–104,
  104–11, 112 *see also* bishops

Printed in the United States
87025LV00007B/4-24/A